200.—

NOTAR

Behind the Smile:
Voices of Thailand

Behind the Smile :
Voices of Thailand
by Sanitsuda Ekachai

For my two mentor journalists - my parents

Behind the Smile:
Voices of Thailand
by Sanitsuda Ekachai

© The Post Publishing Co., Ltd.
ISBN 974-85666-8-4
First published 1990
Reprinted 1991,1992,1993

Published by Thai Development Support Committee
530 Soi St Louis 3
South Sathorn Road
Yannawa
Bangkok 10120
THAILAND

Author and photographer: Sanitsuda Ekachai
Coordinator: Ranee Hassarungsee
Editor: Sarah Sexton
Secretary: Veena Imprasertsuk
Designer: Pracha Suveeranont
Typesetter and production: Dear Book Co., Ltd.
Printer: Samsaen Printing

The articles in *Behind the Smile: Voices
of Thailand* were first printed in the
Bangkok Post. The publishers would
like to thank the *Bangkok Post* for
permission to reproduce them and
CUSO/Thailand for sponsoring their
publication in this book .

Contents

Foreword

Thailand is rapidly and fundamentally changing. Once known as an agricultural country, it started industrialising some 30 years ago, a process which has accelerated in the past few years. Thailand is now tipped to join the ranks of the Newly Industrialising Countries to which its neighbours, Hong Kong, Taiwan, Singapore and South Korea, already belong.

Thai society has gradually been transformed by this industrialisation and modernisation. Changes in traditional economic and social systems, much of them rooted in rural life, have accelerated recently as well. The rapid and often forced pace of this change has had enormous social and economic consequences, not all of them positive. It is ordinary Thai villagers who have borne the brunt of them.

Although praises are sung for the country's economic progress, alongside the advances are stark poverty and an ever-increasing gap between the rich and the poor. The transformation is sweeping along, pushing the poor aside. Despite industrialisation, three-quarters of the Thai population still live in the countryside, trying to make a living off the land. The vast changes to their traditional lifestyle have

occurred within just one generation, exacerbated by landlessness and the breakdown of culture and family relationships. Environmental destruction has been devastating.

Why is this happening? Why are so many people falling
behind? Without understanding these problems, rural dis-
ruption cannot be averted. The persistent and aggravated deterioration of the rural areas in turn causes other social problems, such as city slums and the urban poor, crime, prostitution and child abuse - all of which are on the increase. The
Thai government has tried to solve rural poverty over the past
three decades, but without success.

But how are rural villagers themselves coping with
these vast changes? What do they think are the causes of the
difficulties they face? What are their ideas to do something
about them?

Few people venture out to find the answers. Sanitsuda
Ekachai is an exception. She went to villages in three major
regions of Thailand and heard, first-hand, what rural people
had to say. Her resulting series of articles, published here,
record the changing face of Thailand from the perspective of
rural Thai villagers. They tell of the resourcefulness she found

in their daily struggle to survive and of the humour and sadness as they do so. They reflect Sanitsuda's excellent and compassionate understanding of the complex and interwoven human, social and ecological issues involved, and her ability to communicate this.

Sanitsuda herself says that as a result of her visits and conversations with so many villagers, she has come to respect their sound wisdom, wisdom which may itself provide answers to the many problems Thailand faces, if we only listen to it.

Behind the Smile: Voices of Thailand *enables you to do so.*

Dr Prawase Wasi

Chairperson
Local Development Institute
Bangkok

Notes on Thai words

Ai   a term of respect for an older man, but not as old as one's father

ao moe   Traditionally, there was no paid labour in Thai villages. Activities that required a large number of workers were carried out by a cooperative village work force on a mutual exchange basis. Neighbours pooled together to work for a household which needed its fields planted or harvested or a house built. The members of the household would in turn work for their neighbours.

Baan   means village. Village life is the epitome of Thai traditions and society. A village will usually consist of about 100-150 households with an average of 500-700 inhabitants. Houses are usually built on either side of a road or track which goes through the village. They are built on stilts out of wood, or bamboo and palm leaves. There are an estimated 60,000 villages in Thailand.

A village is the smallest administrative unit in Thailand. Several villages make up a sub-district (*tambon*), which in turn make up a district (*amphur*). A number of districts make up a province (*jangwat*), the largest administrative area in Thailand, of which there are 73 in the country. The provincial town usually has the same name as the province.

baht   the Thai unit of currency. There are 100 satang in one baht. At current exchange rates, one US dollar is equivalent to 25 baht.

Bung   a title which indicates a Muslim man

chao nai   means masters, but is often used by rural people to describe those from the city or town

din   earth

Imam   see *Toh Imam*

kamnan   the sub-district head, elected by villagers in the sub-district

khon muang   the town or city people

khon tai   the southern people

koh   island

laab   a northeastern salad of meat, ground up with vegetables and spices, served with fresh cabbage, mint, cucumber or green beans

luang poh   a term of respect for an older monk, roughly equivalent to Reverend Father

Mae   means mother, pronounced similar to the French mère, but is used to address any older woman

mae yai   a term of respect in the Northeast for an elderly woman

Mah   the southern equivalent of *mae*

pak   vegetable

Phii   spirit. An ancient animist culture preceded Buddhism in Thailand, traits of which persist at many levels of Thai society. Many people still maintain the custom of worshipping and believing in spirits, which are usually considered to be surly beings who are jealous of humans, but have power over what goes on in the universe. A spirit is born out of the soul of a human being who has died. Thais see no contradiction in being Buddhist and believing in spirits.

Phii Sua Baan the spirit which protects a village and looks after its well-being. This spirit will be invoked for prosperity and a good harvest in the village.

Phii Pu Ya the ancestral spirits, similar to the spirits of the first man and woman to inhabit the earth from whom everyone is descended, according to Thai folklore

phii pop a malevolent spirit which feeds on the kidneys and entrails of the body in which it resides. If it is not exorcised, the body wastes away and dies.

pla fish

Poh means father, but is used to address any older man

poh luang a term of respect in the North for elderly men

Pra Kru a term of respect for a low-ranking monk

qateb the deputy religious leader in a Muslim community

rai the Thai unit of measurement of land. One *rai* is approximately 1,600 square metres or two-fifths of an acre.

somtam a traditional northeastern salad, made from raw unripe papaya, chilli and tomatoes to which dry shrimps, salty crabs and peanuts are sometimes added

tuk-tuk a small, three-wheeled, motorised taxi

thao kae Chinese business community

Toh Imam the religious leader in a Muslim community, but as secular affairs are often closely connected, he also acts as village leader

wah another unit of measurement. One *wah* is equivalent to two metres.

wai the Thai greeting. A *wai* is primarily an act of respect which is used on occasions as a greeting as well. To make a *wai*, the palms of the hands are pressed together, fingers pointing upwards, and the head lowered to meet the hands.

Voices from Isan

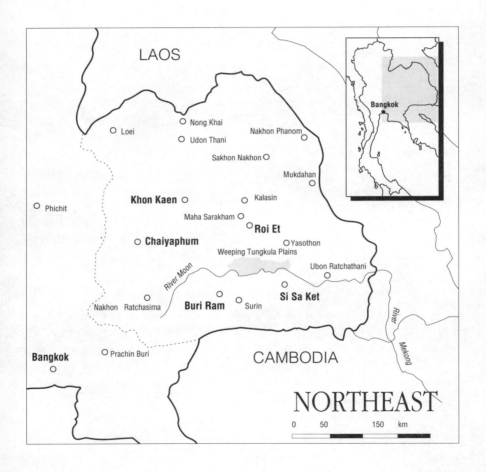

LAOS

Bangkok

Loei
Nong Khai
Udon Thani
Nakhon Phanom
Sakhon Nakhon
Mukdahan
Khon Kaen
Kalasin
Phichit
Maha Sarakham
Roi Et
Chaiyaphum
Yasothon
Weeping Tungkula Plains
Ubon Ratchathani
River Moon
Nakhon Ratchasima
Buri Ram
Surin
Si Sa Ket
Bangkok
Prachin Buri
CAMBODIA
River Mekong

NORTHEAST

0   50   150   km

Voices from Isan

The distinctive Northeast is often called the most traditional part of Thailand. It is culturally close to its neighbours Laos and Cambodia with many people speaking Lao, a language similar to Thai.

The Northeast, known in Thai as Isan, is the largest region of the country, accounting for one third of Thailand's land area. It covers 170,000 square kilometres and is divided into 17 administrative provinces.

An estimated 18 million people live in the Northeast, making up 35 per cent of the Thai population and making Isan the most populous region of the country. Most of them are subsistence farmers. Approximately eight million people live in reserved forest areas in Thailand, most of them in the Northeast, but without legal rights to do so.

Health and educational standards have improved in Isan in the past two or three decades, although the Northeast consistently has the highest levels of child malnutrition in the country. But it is becoming more difficult for people to survive off the land alone, especially with the food and foraging source of the tropical forest gone. Economic disparities between the urban centres and the rural areas continue to grow. The Northeast has the lowest annual per capita income in Thailand, an estimated 5,800 baht (US $235) compared with 25,000 baht (US $1,000) in Bangkok in 1989.

Isan has always been drier and less fertile than other regions of

Thailand, but drought, localised rather than uniform, is now a regular feature of the area. Less than half of the region receives sufficient rain for agriculture.

A contributing factor to erratic and fewer rainfalls has been the clearing of the tropical forest over the past two to three decades to grow cash crops, such as maize, tobacco and tapioca, which is mainly sold to the animal feed markets of the European Economic Community. The loss of the forest has also caused soil erosion, lowering the quality and fertility of the land still further.

When they can, villagers grow one crop of rain-fed rice annually, but need about 15-20 *rai* per family to grow enough for their own needs for the year.

The growing of cash crops has largely replaced the mixture of crops traditionally used for local subsistence. The drop in prices for these crops in recent years has made poverty-related problems worse for most rural communities.

Most are locked into a cycle of debt, borrowing money for intensive modern agriculture - machinery and chemical fertilisers and pesticides - and for basics such as food, housing and clothing. Added to their expenses is the desire for consumer goods which has swept through Isan as through the rest of the country.

Poor yields and low crop prices make it difficult to pay off even the interest on debts, so many farmers take out yet more loans or increase their area of cultivation in the hope of earning more.

Another option is to find work elsewhere. Up to 85 per cent of Isan villagers earn less than they need to survive, so an average of two million people leave their homes each year to work elsewhere. They go to other provinces in the region or further afield in Thailand, while some go abroad to countries such as Singapore and those in the Middle East. Most of those who migrate for less than a year are under 30 years old, although women tend to be younger. Isan is the major source of labour for Bangkok factories.

Like drought, labour migration is now a feature of Isan life, but it has become harder for migrants to earn money in the city because of low wages and the high cost of living, combined with exploitative working conditions.

Yet another alternative that many farmers are turning to is integrated farming. In its most popular form, fishponds are dug in the ricefields where fish can be raised throughout the year. During the rice planting season, they can live in the flooded ricefields while fertilising the rice and eating insects at the same time. Vegetables and fruit trees are grown around the fishpond.

This kind of agriculture reduces the need for expenditure on agricultural production and food, thereby reducing the likelihood of debt.

A growing population and increased cultivation of crops for sale rather than family consumption has meant that all suitable arable land in the Northeast is now under cultivation, although many villagers do not have legal rights to this land. Pressure for land has been exacerbated by the demands of Thai and foreign businesses for land for large-scale eucalyptus tree plantations. Until recently, people outside of Isan were not particularly interested in acquiring or using the land because of its poor quality.

Two aspects of these tree farms concern Isan rural communities: the damage to other crops and the soil, and the appropriation of their land to make way for the plantations.

Using the environmental umbrella, eucalyptus plantations have been encouraged as part of the government's reafforestation policy to raise forest cover up to 40 per cent of the country's land mass from its official current level of 28 per cent.

But 25 per cent of the target has been designated economic or commercial forest - in practice eucalyptus tree farms - and only 15 per cent natural tropical forest. Planted by domestic and multinational companies in areas designated as reserved or degraded forest, the fast-growing tress are cut down after five years for the expanding export markets for paper pulp in Japan, South Korea and Taiwan.

In response to this drive to plant eucalyptus, Isan people have asked the government to grant villagers living in forest reserves rights to use the land, as long as they do not encroach further on any natural forest; to revoke concessions to private companies to plant eucalyptus trees in degraded forest areas where local people now live; and to allow local people to handle reafforestation projects, as long as the trees are not eucalyptus. They have asked the government to distinguish between commercial forestry and replanting of the natural forest.

Villagers are increasingly trying to recover and preserve the forest for themselves as well.

Thanks are due to the following organisations for their assistance with *Voices from Isan*:
    Appropriate Technology Association, Roi Et
    Foundation for Children's Development, Si Sa Ket
    Grass Roots Integrated Development Project, Roi Et
    Integrated Farming Promotion Project, Roi Et
    North East Thailand Development Foundation, Surin
    Press Development Institute of Thailand
    Press Foundation of Asia
    Project for Ecological Recovery, Bangkok
    Resources Sharing for Community Development, Khon Kaen
    Thai Inter-Religious Commission for Development, Surin
    Union for Civil Liberty, Ubon Ratchathani
    and to: Wat Pa Sukato, Chaiyaphum
        Bamrung Boonpanya

Silence in the village

I t is again that time of year when the village is all but deserted.

Most of the able-bodied adults of *Baan* Nongkham in Khon Kaen province have gone to work in sugarcane plantations in the western provinces of Kanchanaburi, Prachuab Khiri Khan and Ratchaburi. Only the elder folk and young mothers with small children remain behind.

"The lorry caravans left just last week," says an old peasant named Iam Pohngarm, sitting on the ground and flicking an old cloth at the insects humming around his dark, wrinkled face.

"My daughters went. My relatives too. Whole families are gone. Old people like me stay behind to look after their shacks."

As in many northeastern villages after the rice harvest in January, a deadly silence is falling upon the nearly empty settlement as the young families leave to sell their labour elsewhere.

These seasonal migrants will return home when the next rice planting season begins in May, if the rains are punctual. That was not the case last year, which explains why the village is emptier than ever.

Drought persisted until November. When the rains eventually came, they were sparing.

"We watched the dark clouds come and relentlessly pass us by," says 70-year-old *Poh* Nuan Mardpanya, the oldest villager in *Baan* Nongkham. "It was the worst drought in ten years."

Except for three families, no one in the village planted rice last year because of the drought.

"Our barns are empty. There's no rice to

▼ *Poh* Iam
Pohngarm

eat, so we have to do whatever we can to survive," says *Poh* Nuan with a tired look in his eyes.

Ironically, this year's high rice price comes at a time when the farmers do not have any rice of their own to eat, let alone sell.

"For me, it means I have to buy the most expensive rice of my life," says *Poh* Nuan.

In this village of 40 households, half of the inhabitants are landless, so their main occupation is as wage labourers.

This year, the drought has forced most of the villagers to join the plantation lorries which came to take Isan workers from their villages to the sugarcane fields.

"We can't find other jobs. We don't know anyone else. If we go to work for the plantation, at least we don't have to pay for transport. They pick us up in January and take us home in April. Every baht counts," explains *Poh* Iam.

Whole families have departed for the plantations. Houses lie hauntingly empty on both sides of the dusty, orange path through the village.

Suk Soitong, his wife and four children all went, taking their pots, pans and rice stock with them because the workers have to cook for themselves.

Poh Jan Penkong went with his eldest son. Widow Joey Boonmee and her four children have gone.

Poh Iam points to two empty shacks near his house. "Two of my daughters and sons-in-law took their children along. I tried to convince them to stay, but they said they needed the money," he says, shaking his head wearily.

Sugarcane cutters have to contend with the hot sun and blade-sharp leaves. They receive 30 baht for every 100 canes they cut.

"Some people can bring home as much as two thousand baht, but many become indebted to the plantation owners for food

"Being in debt is like being entangled in a net. You can't cut yourself loose."

▼ *Pob* Iam
Pohngarm

and rice. So they have to go back again the following year to work to pay off their debts," says *Pob* Iam. "It's like being entangled in a net. You can't cut yourself loose."

There are hardly any young people left in the village. Unlike married couples, who prefer to work on the sugarcane plantations so that they can return home to plant rice, the youngsters seek more permanent work. They only come back once a year for Chinese New Year in January or the Songkhran Festival, the traditional Thai New Year, in April.

"My daughter does housework in Bangkok and my son works in a factory," says landless farmer *Mae* Tee Boonnaree, her teeth stained red from chewing betel and her old clothes stained with dirt.

"They send back money to buy rice. My husband and my eldest son have gone to the sugarcane fields, so I'm left alone with my two small children."

She laughs at herself as she admits to often being reduced to begging other villagers for work as a field hand.

▼ **The old and the young are left behind in Nongkham**

▼ Silk weaving

"It's a hard living. You have to work so hard before you can get something from others to keep your life going."

Although only 60 kilometres from the provincial town of Khon Kaen, *Baan* Nongkham is almost cut off from the outside world. A single, narrow dirt track passes through the village, a track which turns into a stream of muddy wallows when the rains come.

"It used to be a thick forest here, and the rains were more regular," recalls *Poh* Nuan as he looks around at the bare ricefields, sparsely dotted with trees under the vast skies.

One of the villagers' dreams is electricity. Flickering gas lamps are now the only source of light after dark. It's hardly enough to read by, but then, no one can afford to buy newspapers.

Radios are the most convenient connection with the outside world. The buffalo boys and girls clutch these precious possessions as they watch their charges grazing in the fields.

With little to do after the harvest, the shirtless men in their sarongs squat beside the dirt path, elbows on their knees, sucking at blades of grass as they talk.

Equally oblivious of the passage of time are the women at their looms, lost in the hypnotic movements of their weaving which preserve them from straying thoughts and fears of what the future might bring.

As the orange rays of sunset begin to blush the skies, the buffalo herds head back home. A large group of children, dressed in rags, watch the village's only working television, run off a car battery at the grocery shop. The buffaloes plod past the empty houses to their byres under their owners' high stilted houses.

Poh Nuan solemnly watches another day passing, a blank expression on his face.

"Life seems to get worse," he says. "Fathers, mothers, sons, daughters, we can no longer afford to stay together. We live day-to-day, taking things as they come. We just hope we will struggle through." ■

Dangers of working in Bangkok

Sood Srisuwan, aged 44, used to work in Bangkok as a poultry slaughterer. After one year, he came back home - mad.

His 37-year-old brother, Tong, worked as a taxi driver. He returned home after an accident - paralysed.

Former *tuk-tuk* driver Sua Mukdadee, aged 49, lives in another world. He sits all day in front of the buffaloes, staring into space. He has been like that for more than ten years since he came back from the city.

With drooping head and eyes full of worry, 47-year-old Boonma Sawansopa, another taxi driver, suffers from hallucinations and headaches.

"But I have to go back to Bangkok again," he says. "I have to work to support my family."

There are risks beyond disablement in accidents or robberies for men working in Bangkok. Mental casualties are high in the small village of only 40 families of Don Samran in Roi Et province. But that does not stop the

▼ Jamrat Jamsena,
village head of
Don Samran
▼ ▼ Jamrat Jamsena
and his extended
family

villagers setting out for Bangkok after the rice harvest to find work.

"It's the horse medicine that killing us," says village head Jamrat Jamsena, aged 39, referring to the stimulants drivers and poultry slaughterers take to help them keep going through the long working hours 'with the strength of horses.'

From among its yellow seas of dry ricefields, *Baan* Don Samran, like other northeastern villages, sends its migrant workers to the same occupations in Bangkok, a sort of transplanted village guild. Theirs is a village of poultry slaughterers and *tuk-tuk* drivers who, with

time and experience, become taxi drivers.

"Most taxi drivers in Bangkok come from Roi Et province," says village head Jamrat. "For many of us, it is just hopping from a buffalo's back to a steering wheel."

Newcomers pay experienced drivers about 80 baht a day to teach them how to drive, explains Jamrat. Lesson time is around

three or four in the morning near the Royal Plaza, when the dimly-lit streets are nearly empty.

"Then off we go to hit the Bangkok streets! We might not have the experience, but we sure have the guts."

They use the horse medicine, sometimes called diligence medicine, to overcome fear as well as drowsiness, especially when driving at night.

"We've had lots of accidents and robberies," says the village head, himself a retired taxi driver, "but no one from our village has been killed so far, thank goodness."

The poultry slaughterers all go to work in the same place in Bangkok's Chinatown.

Until two years ago, 50-year-old Sood Srikam was the connection between his fellow villagers of *Baan* Don Samran and the bosses of the slaughter houses. He was in charge of giving the horse medicine to the workers.

Now a weakened figure left at home in

▼ Sua Mukdadee

the village, the strong smell of alcohol exudes from him as he speaks of his work and what happened to those he was in charge of.

"It was my job to make the slaughterers work hard. Without the medicine, they can't work. You should see them when they wake up. They can't do a thing. But the medicine works wonders. I took it too. It was my job. Otherwise, the owner would scold me."

After a day's work using stimulants, the workers are too active to go to sleep. They need alcohol to shut down the working machine. Year after year, the cumulative effects on the mind of the alcohol, the drugs, or both, can be disastrous.

It was this Sood who gave the horse medicine to his brother-in-law, Sood Srisuwan, for whom the effects were too strong, pushing him into depression, hallucination and finally madness.

Drunk and plagued by guilt, Sood Srikam admits that many of his subordinates became absent minded because of the drug. Then he denies it vehemently. "It was my

"I don't know when we're going to learn our lesson. Maybe it's our empty stomachs that block our clear heads."

▼ **Growing vegetables
is an alternative**

job," he keeps on saying.

Village head Jamrat says he tries to persuade his villagers not to leave for Bangkok, but to no avail.

"No one wants to leave, but we simply have to," he explains. "A lot of us have to pay off the cost of the fertilisers we borrowed for rice farming."

A bag of fertiliser costs around 200 baht at the market. With interest, farmers usually have to pay back around 340 baht for one bag. "I myself quit working in Bangkok a few

years ago," he says. "The risk is so high that it's not worth it any more."

Instead of heading for the city and letting his family back home buy food, he dug a fishpond in his ricefield and began growing vegetables for his family to eat.

"The villagers have adopted a wait-and-see attitude to this kind of farming. They want to be sure that my solution is effective before they follow me. If they were to fail, they would end up starving. It's too high a risk," he explains.

Although he has turned his back on city work, Jamrat is still haunted by his own family tragedy on the migrant trail. His younger brother, another victim of the stimulants, got lost on his way home to the village and has still not been found.

"He had painful headaches and suffered hallucinations," says Jamrat. "My parents sold their house to look for him, but we still don't know where he is."

In the course of their survival, the villagers of *Baan* Don Samran have paid a high price for the benefits they have received from Bangkok. Yet, as the harvest ends, they start heading for the capital again, as they have done for years.

""I don't know when we're going to learn our lesson," says village head Jamrat. "Maybe it's our empty stomachs that block our clear heads." ∎

Family break-up

▼ Buppa Kongtham

Buppa Kongtham vows never to let her children go off to Bangkok, no matter how poor they are. She says she has learnt her lesson.

"It was Bangkok and drugs that killed our family," says the 36-year-old divorcee. "I lost my husband to madness. I lost my marriage. My family is broken in pieces. I never want my children even to risk suffering the same tragedy."

Sood Srisuwan was Buppa's husband, the victim of stimulant drugs who returned home, mad, after working in Bangkok as a poultry slaughterer.

Taking his place as the family breadwinner, Buppa worked in the ricefields, and sold sweets at the village school and at temple fairs up to seven kilometres away. Her husband, meanwhile, lived in another world, listening to strange whispers.

"During those years, I often worked in the fields in tears," she says. "But I kept

"Bangkok and drugs killed our family."

▼ **Buppa's husband,
Sood Srisuwan**

hoping that he would return to normal."

She gave up hope seven years ago when her husband nearly strangled her to death. "That's why I separated from him," she explains. "He was angry with me. The witch doctor hit him several times to try to chase the evil spirits away. I took him there myself. But it was no use."

There is no bitterness in her voice, just fierce determination not to let the same thing happen to her children.

Her son has since married and followed the Isan tradition of moving into his wife's house. Her daughter Kampa, aged 15, takes care of the buffaloes and helps her in the fields.

"I don't know, though, how long I can convince her to stay," says Buppa, switching to the central Thai dialect as soon as her village friends have left the conversation.

"I used to work in Bangkok too, as a maid and a cook, to pay my husband's medical bills," she explains. "It was hard to get used to being bossed around and getting rude scoldings."

Walking long distances under the hot sun to look for food in the fields, fetching brackish water from the village's ponds, sitting at the loom till late at night to make traditional cloth to wear and to sell - these are the ways of life she says she feels more comfortable with.

"Working in the fields is hard, but you feel like a free person," she says.

Her life, like that of other northeastern villagers, centres on getting enough food to eat.

"You look for food during the day to eat in the evening," she says. "You don't have time to think of much else."

Bangkok is still a place to make money, but not a place to stay for a long time, because of the likelihood of discrimination against northeasterners.

"I go to Bangkok only once a year, at Chinese New Year in January, to work as a poultry slaughterer to get some cash," she says, dismissing the fact that she is the only woman in the village team which goes to the city each year for the occasion.

"You can't be too choosy about your work," she says matter-of-factly. "If you are, your children will starve to death." ∎

Child workers return home

Samuan Thonglai is 14 years old. She has just run away from a small home factory that forced her to look for her food in the ricefields.

But she considers herself lucky. At least, she was able to get back, well and uninjured, to her home in Tung Sak village in Si Sa Ket province.

Her friend Jaang Pankaen, also 14, was not so lucky. While looking for small shrimps and clams in the ricefields together with Samuan, Jaang came across a poisonous mollusc and developed a serious rash. Her legs are now pocked with infections and itchy, dark red spots.

Apart from her terrible rash, Jaang may have been working for nothing as well. Her wages are still with her employer, and there is no guarantee now that she will get her hard-earned money.

Jaang, Samuan and four other girls from their village, all sisters and friends, escaped

"If it hadn't been for the bad drought last year, I wouldn't have sent my daughter to work."

▼ Jaang Pankaen
(left) and her
sister Li

mixed feelings. They may be happy and relieved that the girls are home, but their return means a stop to indispensable income - and more mouths to feed.

"If it hadn't been for the bad drought last year, I wouldn't have sent my daughter to work," says Samuan's mother, Pian Thonglai.

"I thought that she would be well treated. After all, we know the employer. He's our neighbour's relative," adds the 43-year-old peasant woman whose red-stained teeth and sickly look make her seem much older.

Jaang's mother, however, could not hide her anger. "You could have waited until

from the home factory which made baby-clothes in the eastern province of Prachin Buri and arrived home a few days ago.

Their parents received the girls with

you got your money at least, not just escape like this. It's money down the drain."

Teachers in the village say children usually stay home for two or three years after

"There is no point in making her stay here. The family will run out of rice soon enough, even without her."

▼ **Future child labourers ?**

finishing their six-year compulsory education at the age of 12 before they go to the city to look for work. Because of last year's droughts, however, 20 out of 25 school-leavers left for Bangkok immediately.

"We only have two sacks of rice left from last year's harvest. That can last us only two or three months more," says *Mae* Pian. About ten sackfuls of rice are usually needed to feed a family of five for a whole year.

Tung Sak is not the only village in the district to suffer from drastically low harvests. In eight other villages, the harvest dropped to less than half of the previous year's production. At nearby *Baan* Keng, most villagers have less than one sack of rice. Not one family has the ten sacks needed to last the whole year.

In these cases, debts increase and more children leave home to bring in the much-needed cash.

Jaang says the problems began when the home factory moved from Bangkok to a town in Prachin Buri to avoid being spotted by tax officials.

"We usually worked from morning till night. We often kept at it the whole night through when it was really urgent. But if we had nothing to sew the next day, we weren't allowed to rest. We had to help with the rice harvesting."

Looking back, Jaang says she did not mind the work. "But they didn't give us enough food. They gave us one kilogramme of boiled mackerel for one week and forced us to find food for ourselves in the fields. It was worse than staying home."

Samuan's homecoming means more debts for her mother and less rice for the family.

"She borrowed from Jaang to pay the bus fare home," explains her mother. "I had to sell some of my rice to pay the debt."

Once bitten, however, the girls are not twice shy about leaving home again to find work.

"We will go again. Not alone, though. We're sticking together," says Jaang.

"I am afraid for my daughter," says Samuan's mother. "But there is no point in making her stay here. The family will run out of rice soon enough, even without her." ∎

Today's menu: ants' eggs, beetles, crickets

Silkworms, grasshoppers, ants' eggs, tadpoles - the list of edibles that nature offers to northeastern peasants is endless. They have learned to relish them in the course of their centuries-long struggle for survival.

In the hot season, when fish are rare and ponds have turned into puddles, those who stay on in the village, rather than going to look for work elsewhere, spend most of their days in the fields or nearby forests looking for food.

"Our life revolves around food hunting," says Jamrat Jamsena, village headman of *Baan* Don Samran in Roi Et province. "You start looking for food early in the morning to have something to eat in the evening, and another day passes by."

Familiar sights along Isan roads indicate the villagers' concern with staying ahead of hunger. Mothers and children are digging the dry earth, looking for who-knows-what. Men are wading in puddles, looking for fish or bullfrogs hidden in the mud, oblivious to the hellish heat. Their tools are simple: experience has refined their skills into an art of survival.

With nature as the boss, the villagers are alive to the slightest change in the weather, as it may mean the mushrooms are sprouting, the frogs returning or the *tao* moss forming, all waiting to be picked up to fill the family cooking pot.

"Except for the biting chill at night, January is relatively kind to us," says Jamrat. "There are still fish in the swamp, and we can always find clams, water snails, tadpoles and different sorts of frogs nearby."

The tadpoles are usually prepared with chilli into a spicy northeastern *laab*, mixed with fermented fish or wrapped in banana leaves and roasted. Frogs are at their best in an *om*, sharing the bowl with ground rice, chilli and any available vegetables.

But tadpoles and frogs, he says, have become increasingly rare because of the use of batteries to catch fish. They electrocute the fish, but kill off frogs and tadpoles as well.

"As for the birds, they return in February and stay until May," reports Jamrat, noting that there have gradually been fewer birds over the years as the forests have disappeared. "More often than not, we spend the whole day

▼ Jamrat Jamsena
catches fish from
the village pond

the same way as crunchy crickets before being eaten, *jeenoon* beetles and nun moths.

"If there is a brief shower of rain during this time, we go out in hordes looking for *jeenoon* beetles," he says. "They come out to eat the sprouting leaves. All we have to do is light fires under the trees, and they just fall off onto the ground."

April, the height of the hot season, means cracked land and fierce heat. It is the time when chicken bones and boiled mackerel are the villagers' main food, together with sticky rice.

"If we don't have enough money, we have to trade our rice for the fish and chicken bones," says Jamrat. "A bucketful of rice can bring us one kilo of mackerel."

in the bush with our shotguns, only to return home empty-handed."

With the March heat, villagers have to turn to looking for ground lizards, edible insects and beetles to compensate for fish, which are harder to find by then.

Until April, it is common to see children digging into the buffalo dung with long sticks, looking for *joodjee* beetles, which are roasted

But if nature is punctual and kind, it will rain lightly in May, and the farmers can start ploughing their ricefields while waiting for more rain to plant the rice paddy.

Apart from grasshoppers and crickets, red ants and ants' eggs are the delicacies of the month.

▼ Collecting food
from the forest

Expert eyes will not miss an ants' nest, hidden in a mass of wilted leaves, glued together like a basket. When the nest is shaken with a long stick, worker ants and their eggs fall out and are caught in a bucket of water, but the hunter-gatherer dashes away in a flash to escape being bitten by them.

The forest is a free market for various kinds of vegetables. The young leaves of mango trees, cassia, neem trees, tamarinds, basils and *mah noi*, the little dog tree, are abundant. The leaves of the *mah noi* are minced with water and turn into a green gelatine which is eaten like *a laab* with hot plums, not limes, from the forest which give it its pleasant sour taste.

All sorts of yams come to the rescue of the villagers' hunger in these months when the rice barn is empty. When collecting yams, Jamrat says the villagers respect the unwritten rule of always putting the climbing stems back on the ground, so that they will grow again to

"The forest is diminishing. The droughts are getting longer, and food is harder to find."

▼ **Boiling silkworms to collect the silk thread**

▼ ▼ **A snack of boiled silkworms**

produce yams for the next year.

"This is very important, because we often have to go without rice during the droughts and depend solely on these yams," he says. "Killing the yam plants is like killing ourselves."

The villagers welcome the August and September storms, which mean all kinds of mushrooms will sprout.

"If no one has been there before us, the mushrooms will be waiting for us in exactly the same places they were the previous years," says Jamrat.

The rain also brings out bamboo shoots which remain abundant until October.

"By this time, the water level in our ricefields will be lower, and women will be

out there catching fish," he says. "A good catch means we can make enough fermented fish to last the whole year, or we can trade them for rice if the harvest is poor."

Apart from fish, there should be plenty of fat rice rats and land crabs. The rats, says Jamrat, are roasted or fried, while the crabs are mixed with the all-time Isan favourite, *somtam* or papaya salad.

When the fish are so small that they go through his fingers, Jamrat says he turns his attention to aquatic weeds such as budding hyacinth, *pak waen*, *pak pipuay*, *tao* moss or, if he is lucky, the hair-like, emerald-green *lindong*, which can only be found in April in the nearby Moon River.

"Hunger is the enemy we still cannot beat."

▼ **Bicyclists going fishing**

After the rice harvest, women go back to their looms to make cloth for family use. In villages where they raise silkworms, villagers munch boiled silkworms, sprinkled with salt, as a snack after they have taken away the cocoon for its silk thread.

Baby kapok fruits with their crunchy texture and mild sweetness are another village favourite, especially among children.

In December, fish can be found only in swamps or rivers. It is common to see hundreds of villagers in rows of bicycles, all heading for the same place to compete for a good catch.

By evening, however, the faces of the bicyclists heading back home from the Moon River indicate that their day-long fishing expedition has not ended satisfactorily.

"The forest is diminishing. The droughts are getting longer, and food is harder too find," says Jamrat. "Hunger is the enemy we still cannot beat." ■

Toads jump the family income

oad hunting is a booming business in *Baan* Song Hong, a small village in Roi Et province.

Despite the commonly-held belief that toads are poisonous to the touch, the fearless *Baan* Song Hong villagers go out in droves to hunt for the ugly animals to sell their skins to wallet and bag makers in Bangkok.

A villager gets one baht for four big toads with tough skins. At least 20,000 toads have met their fate during recent months as poverty and drought have forced villagers to use them to make ends meet.

"I'm not a good hunter," says Moon Karnjak, aged 33, self-effacingly. "The most I can catch is about one hundred a day. The best hunters here can catch as many as four hundred a day."

A village of some one hundred households about 50 kilometres from the provincial town of Roi Et, *Baan* Song Hong is surrounded by vast ricefields.

▼ **Moon Karnjak**

Like other north-eastern villages, the peasants were hit by a serious drought and late rainfall last year. Their small rice stocks will not last long, so they have to do whatever possible to get food.

According to the villagers, the brisk business in toads started about five years ago. As there are now few toads left in their village, the hunters have to walk long distances under the sun to nearby villages to look for them. They say they have not noticed that there are more mosquitoes or other insects in the village as a result of fewer, insect-eating toads.

The buyers generally come to the village in their pick-up trucks to say how many toads they want, and then come back a few days later to collect them.

"We start going out hunting immediately after they've come," says Moon, adding that she often has to walk as far as 13 kilometres a day.

Her hunting continues from dawn until dusk. After cooking sticky rice and packing it in a straw container, she wraps her head with cotton cloth to protect herself from the harsh sun, deftly balances two empty, rattan baskets on her shoulders and off she goes.

The toads' liking for cool places make them easy targets. "We just look for them in cool spots, such as near swamps, in puddles, under trees or even beside the water jars in our houses," she says.

The hunters' best catching equipment is their own bare hands. "No need to use gloves or sticks. You just catch them, just like that," she says. "It is not at all true that touching them causes skin irritation. I just wash my hands with detergent or soap after I finish my work, and my hands are fine," says Moon matter-of-factly, showing her strong, tough, farmer's hands as proof.

"On a lucky day, I can get about twenty-five baht to buy food for my children. But generally I can only make a few baht a day."

The toads are sold to the village grocer, Pian Daodej, who acts as the sole agent for the toad skinners.

"The size doesn't matter," he explains. "As long as the skin is tough and thick, it will do.

"They have ordered more than one hundred thousand this year, but there are fewer and fewer toads in the area, so we have to walk further and further to find them. Last year we only caught about twenty thousand," he says.

The toads are kept in a specially dug hole in front of his shop and fed only with water. They can usually survive for days in the cool hole until the skinners come to collect them.

It is a prosperous business for Pian. He earns one hundred per cent profit by selling the toads to the skinner in a nearby village, who in turn preserves the toad skins with salt before selling them to merchants elsewhere in Roi Et province.

The buyer of the toads, 39-year-old Bua Luejinda, lives about seven kilometres away, but it is his wife who is in charge of the skinning.

"I have to skin them in the ricefields, because the work is so smelly and bloody," she says.

She cuts off the toads' legs and heads and takes out their intestines before preserving them with salt.

In a corner of her shack stands a metre-tall, traditional ceramic jar containing more than 6,000 pungent-smelling toad skins, ready to be sent off to another village in Roi Et where they are dried before being sent to Bangkok to be made into leather for stylish wallets and bags.

The farmer couple say they get a commission of 500 to 600 baht for every thousand toad skins.

"I earn about twenty to thirty thousand baht a year from the commission," says Bua beaming. "The money comes in very handy, especially when the rice harvest is bad because of the drought."

It is noticeable, however, that only middle-aged villagers are involved in the toad business.

"Most youngsters leave the village for Bangkok to find work. Those of us who are left behind are young mothers with small children or older people," says Moon, herself a mother of five. "Catching toads is our small way of making extra cash."

Some teenage boys keep clear of the amphibians, saying that they are still afraid of what they believe is the poisonous toad skin. Others, however, have a more personal explanation.

"What if the girls in the other villages saw me running around after toads?" asks one buffalo boy shyly. "That wouldn't make much of a first impression, would it?"   ■

Cashing in on religious robes

▼ Mee Naewprasert
and his wife

I t started off as a quick way to make money while sacrificing basic values. But posing as monks and nuns is now a new occupation for thousands of poor farmers in Chaiyaphum and nearby provinces.

"I know this is sinful and I'm afraid I'll go to hell," says Poon Patchakiao, a young mother of three. "But everyone is doing it and everyone is making a fortune. It would be stupid not to do the same."

Dressed in white and with her head shaven as nuns have to be, Poon was arrested together with 18 other fake nuns and monks in the first police raid since the fraud began five years ago in the area.

Poon lives in Nong Ta Na, a village of some 100 households where most of the villagers are cashing in on the bogus cleric racket. After friends and relatives in two adjacent villages made a fortune through such impostures, her village followed suit.

Ironically, one of the neighbouring villages that Nong Ta Na took after was cited by authorities last year in a nationwide campaign as a village free of vice .

"I know this is sinful and I'm afraid I'll go to hell. But I need money to pay debts and buy rice."

▼ **Fake nuns arrested**

Not so long ago, Poon remembers, villagers threw dust at bogus monks who walked past their homes. They cursed them as mad ghosts who contaminated the sacred, saffron robes they wore.

The mad ghosts, however, came back with the kind of money that could free them of their debts, buy new ricefields and build new houses. Some sported status items such as motorcycles. Poon, understandably, wavered.

"I gave it a lot of thought," she says. "I felt ashamed, but it was all very tempting. The teacher's wife did it. The headman's wife, too. And who am I? Just a nobody. I need money to pay debts and buy rice even more than they do," she reasoned.

According to *Pra Kru* Pisalchaiyakhun, the chief monk of the district, this lucrative business has spread to other villages in Chaiyaphum and nearby provinces. He sees no effective means of stopping it, because the saffron robe is still very much revered by the general public.

Bogus nuns are a recent phenomenon, he says. Men started the trend by disguising themselves as monks by putting on the saffron-coloured robes and shaving their heads to ask for food and donations in Bangkok.

Women simply followed their example.

"I had to invest, too," says Poon. "Two to three hundred baht for the fake certificates which say I'm a nun and more than eight hundred baht for the nun's white robes and gear."

In return for approximately the same amount of money, men are generally able to solicit 3,000 to 10,000 baht a month in donations, while women can get only about 2,000 or 3,000 baht, because nuns are held to be inferior to monks and often looked down upon.

Jobless after the rice harvest, middle-aged and old villagers who cannot sell their labour elsewhere find that the fake monk and nun business suits them perfectly. This is where it is better, for once, to be older.

Poon's husband brought home only 500 baht after working as a labourer in Bangkok for several months, whereas an elderly monk-imposter might get a few thousand in a matter of weeks without having to lift a finger.

Before being arrested, Poon asked her husband to cease his visits to Bangkok and allow her to support the family instead.

At the police station, 29-year-old Poon is the youngest of the fake nuns, most of whom are in their ripe old age.

"It will be a never-ending game of cat and mouse as long as the root problem of poverty is not solved."

Eyes downcast, mouths stained from chewing betel nuts, theirs are the same wrinkled old faces which can be seen in most northeastern villages where the driving force in life is to find enough food for the next meal.

Sympathisers view the bogus cleric racket as the villagers' way of 'beating the system' which, in their opinion, helps the wealthy and influential to rob the weak and the poor through sophisticated schemes.

The reverend abbot *Pra Kru* Pisalchaiyakhun, however, disagrees. "This is an issue of greed. There are many poor villagers who do not need to resort to such fraudulence for survival."

With new-found affluence, gambling is widespread in Poon's small village. Alcohol-related problems have increased. Farmers' respect for the village abbot has declined following his pleas that they stop posing as bogus monks and nuns.

"Once they threatened to tear down the community hall, because I called a meeting asking villagers to stop this cheating," he says. "They angrily told me to mind my own business. I was not the one to help them in times of hunger, they said."

A Chaiyaphum policeman admits feeling heavy-hearted at having to arrest elderly villagers on charges of deceit.

"It will be a never-ending game of cat and mouse as long as the root problem of poverty is not solved," he says.

In a decrepit shack in nearby Nong Kham village, an emaciated landless farmer, Mee Naewprasert, aged 58, says he and his wife only go to Bangkok when they run out of rice.

"I don't know the city very well. I just tag along with a group," he says, fear showing through his clouded eyes. Like many others in the village, he wears a knitted hat to cover his bare, shaven head. A ragged piece of cloth, torn from an old saffron robe, has been left to dry, blowing about in the wind outside.

"When I have enough to buy a sack of rice, I come back home. I don't want much," adds his wife, a tiny, withered-looking woman in tattered clothes.

But on the dirt street outside, two sturdy young men with shaven heads are enjoying a bicycle ride. Unlike the elderly Naewprasert couple who look scared, these two turn hostile at seeing strangers intruding upon their territory.

In a village of fake monks and nuns, you certainly could not expect to find the usual aura of friendliness and hospitality prevalent in most rural areas.

"Villagers have changed tremendously," says *Pra Kru* Pisalchaiyakhun sighing. "It is true that the villagers are poor and need a lot of support. But I am still against the idea of using one's poverty to justify fraudulence and greed." ■

Trees of our choice

◄ *Mae* Kongsri
Sopawet
▼ *Mae* Kongsri
Sopawet by the
eucalyptus
plantation

O nly ten years ago, farmer Kongsri Sopawet and her family were told by the authorities to stay put in the Dong Yai reserved forest to fight off the communists and help establish a stable community.

The conflicts have now died down, but their victory has led to another battle. This time it is the authorities themselves who are the enemy, a new threat to their land.

No longer needed, *Mae* Kongsri and nearly 1,300 families from 19 villages in the district were told to pack up and go, because the formerly communist-infiltrated forestland in the mountainous water catchment area was needed for commercial eucalyptus planting in accordance with the national reafforestation programme.

"Is this what you get for fighting for your country?" moans the 50-year-old *mae yai* who has lost all her land. "Is this what you get for risking your life for years?"

Despite feeling used and cheated, the villagers are resisting being swept off the ideological chess board on which they have been pawns, now that the first match is over.

They are demanding not to be cut out of the tree planting scheme and are refusing to move. They are preparing rubber saplings to plant where officials plan to put in eucalyptus trees.

"We are willing to cooperate with the reafforestation policy," says Charn Somaboot, village head of *Baan* Teppattana in Buri Ram province. "But why can't we choose trees that will benefit us villagers as well?"

Baan Teppattana, where *Mae* Kongsri lives, was one of the defence volunteer villages supported by the Thai Army in its efforts to counter infiltration by communist guerrillas in what was then the dense Dong Yai forest.

Fleeing from drought in their old homes in the northeastern provinces of Ubon Ratchathani and Roi Et, they moved to the area about 30 years ago, looking for fertile land.

"We were encouraged to burn down trees, so that the guerrillas could not make use of the forest," says *Mae* Kongsri. "We were given plots of land to till as well."

Village legends are rich with tales of

▼ **Guarding the
  rubber trees**

their own head-hunting unit, their tense life under arms and their various tactics to counter the guerrillas' attacks - all to protect their land.

At the height of the fighting during 1978 and 1979, the Teppattana villagers recall with pride how they fought, both men and women, shoulder-to-shoulder with the Army.

"We went along with the troops for days because we knew the territory better," says *Mae* Kongsri. "Men were recruited to join the military's own guerrilla unit. We women helped with the food. No one can claim that

they could have won the battle without our villagers' sweat and blood."

But in 1984, the villagers were ordered to move out of the reserved forest they had settled in to make room for commercial planting of eucalyptus trees.

Government officials offered land allotments to compensate only about 300 of the 1,300 families living in the area. To make matters worse, the villagers say that some of these allotments infringed on the farmland of other villagers.

"What the officials did was to tell us to go ahead and farm on someone else's property, just like that," complains *Mae* Kongsri. "Is this part of a plan to make us villagers kill each other?"

Armed with information and united in determination, the villagers point out that, according to the law, commercial forestry needs community consent and the workers must be local people in accordance with the project's job-creation objective.

"The fact is, this deal did not pass our sub-district council, and the workers are from other provinces," says village head Charn.

At the height of the conflict, an angry mob cut down eucalyptus saplings and commandeered bulldozers. Petitions were sent to the military in the area and to the provincial governor. The sub-district council agreed to oppose the eucalyptus plantation and to

"Why can't we reach a deal that will benefit us both, so the country can regain its forests and we can still earn a living to survive?"

replace it with rubber trees instead.

But the result has been a deadlock. Villagers now guard their rubber nursery with carbines and once again live under the stress and strain they felt in the years of fighting the communists.

Nobody can tell what will happen when villagers insist on planting rubber while the Forestry Department presses on with its plans to extend the commercial eucalyptus project.

As villagers stand ready to defend their land against further eucalyptus planting, the fast plunge into poverty and hardship which *Mae* Kongsri has suffered is a living warning of what could happen to them if they lose the struggle.

Mae Kongsri has lost her orchard and tapioca fields to the first phase of the eucalyptus plantation in this water catchment area. Despite promises of help, she has still not received any land compensation.

"I still remember vividly the bulldozers destroying my orchard, my mangoes, my jackfruits, my sweet tamarind trees. They took away my land, my only property," she says, her eyes reddened. "I could not sleep for worry. It is so unfair."

She has sold her house to pay off her debts, built a small shack on a piece of land up on the hill and joined the wage-earning class, considered the poorest of the poor among the villagers.

The old woman is allowed to plant tapioca between rows of young eucalyptus trees, but she says her income has dropped drastically from 8,000 to 1,500 baht a year because of poor yields.

To prove her point, she digs up a full-grown tapioca plant to reveal a thin, unhealthy tuber, strangled by the vigorous roots of the eucalyptus trees.

Of her orchard, there remains only one jackfruit tree which *Mae* Kongsri, desperate to hold on to her property, asked forestry officials to spare. An island in the hot, dry eucalyptus plot, the tree's shade is now the only cool spot where her husband can rest from planting tapioca between the rows of eucalyptus. *Mae* Kongsri herself refuses to work there, saying that she could not stand the pain.

She says she agrees with the village's plea to pay rent for their land in the reserved forest to grow fruit or rubber trees there to keep the place green.

"Why can't we reach a deal that will benefit us both, so the country can regain its forests, and we, the villagers, can still earn a living to survive?" asks the old woman, looking wistfully at the hundreds of jackfruits on the tree above her.

"We are poor people. Don't you think we should be able at least to grow what we can eat?" ∎

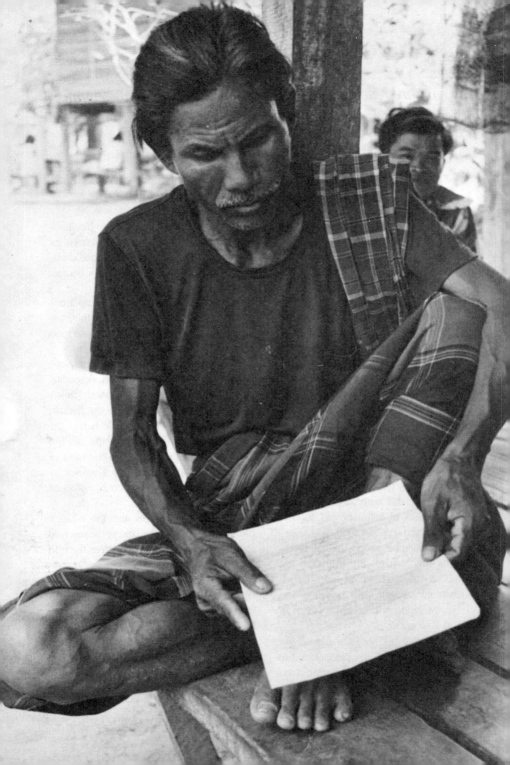

Standing up to the authorities

◄ *Pob* Onn Wattanap-rom

▼ Village head Supote Kitsawat (right) and *Pob* Onn on their village's public grazing land

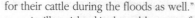

I n just one week, villagers in *Baan* Toey in Roi Et province saved their grazing grounds from being turned into a plantation of euca-lyptus trees.

"You have to act immediately before they can get their hands on the fields," says village head Supote Kitsawat, explaining the tactics he used to save the village's 278 *rai* of common land. "Once the eucalyptus saplings are planted, things get too complicated. The other side won't budge for fear of losing face."

The crisis occurred last year when the Forestry Department attempted to add commercial value to the dry, weed-strewn common outside the village.

"To outsiders, it may look like a wasteland during the dry season. But wait until the rainy season when the floods come," says Supote. "This is the only place above the level of the water where we can keep our cattle."

Like other villages along the Moon River, *Baan* Toey is flooded for up to four or five months of the year during the rainy season when the river bursts its low banks.

"In our village alone, we have more than two thousand buffaloes which have to be kept on the high ground. And more than ten villages around here use this land as a refuge for their cattle during the floods as well."

A village island in the golden seas of dry, rice stems after the harvest, *Baan* Toey is on the southern fringe of the Weeping Tungkula Plains, the vast, arid flatland which extends into ten districts of five provinces in the Northeast.

Because of the area's legendary aridity, there have been concerted government efforts to develop it in a project known as the Greening of Isan. The fast-growing eucalyptus tree is believed to be a quick way of turning the brown fields into green forest.

"People talk so much about the dryness of the Weeping Tungkula Plains," says village head Supote. "Ten years ago, it was true, we would not want to live and farm here. But that was before cheap chemical fertiliser reached the countryside."

The formerly empty plains have now been occupied by rice farmers. Although their yield is not as good as elsewhere, it is enough to meet basic necessities, if the weather is kind.

When the eucalyptus project reached *Baan* Toey in July 1987, the villagers had no idea what was going on until tractors were on the common.

Armed with spades and mere sticks, the

"How do they expect their commercial forest to survive without community support?"

whole village rushed to the scene to stop what they saw as an invasion of their rightful property.

"Even the children joined in," recalls the village head. "Everyone was so angry that I thought they would turn violent. I had to calm them down before any blood was shed."

That same day, the village sent a protest to the sub-district office where they discovered that the project had not even been approved by the sub-district council.

Within a week, the council refused permission for the public grazing land to be turned into state commercial forest, ending the conflict once and for all.

Apart from swift action, information is necessary for a successful strategy against such a plantation, adds another village leader, 54-year-old *Poh* Onn Wattanaprom.

For the past ten years, he explains, a large expanse of land elsewhere in the Weeping Tungkula Plains has been used for a commercial eucalyptus plantation. Villagers there have noticed changes in the soil and realised the effects of losing their rights over their land.

"We have friends and relatives in that area," says *Poh* Onn. "They have warned us against this dangerous tree. It hardens the land, consumes so much water and its roots kill other trees and plants nearby."

Word has also spread that officials do not necessarily keep their promises that cattle will be allowed to graze in the eucalyptus plantations.

"We were told a fence would be put up around the forest to prevent trespassing, but this would keep the cattle out as well. Besides, after the eucalyptus trees have been growing for a few years, there isn't any grass under them any more, so we can't make use of our old land anyway."

Poh Onn and village head Supote are urging officials to use trees indigenous to Thailand such as *keelek, taad* and tamarind in the state reafforestation scheme rather than the Australian eucalyptus.

"It's a misunderstanding that our soil in the Weeping Tungkula Plains is so poor that trees can't grow here," says Supote, pointing to rows of *taad* trees among the fields.

His village of some 200 families is surrounded by a fringe of tall trees, so that from afar, it looks like an island oasis amid the vast fields.

"The trees can grow very well, if we dig the land and turn the topsoil over," he adds. "But this needs time and energy, and we need help in this respect. We hope that, in future, officials will ask us first what we know and what we need. How else can they get accurate information? And how do they expect their commercial forest to survive without community support?" ∎

Trees cut down . . . to plant trees

▼ *Pob* Siri
Jamhinkong

A t the age of 75, retired teacher Siri - Jamhinkong decided it was time for him to stand up and fight.

To protect his village's forest, the lanky and ailing old man led hundreds of angry villagers from *Baan* Nam Kham in Roi Et province to protest against the official de-struction of their trees to make way for a government reafforestation project of euca-lyptus trees.

"It was ridiculous," says the village leader. "Why cut down trees to plant trees? Why destroy an important source of food and medicine? City people never understand how

▼ **A forest destroyed**

That was nearly two years ago. After a mass protest, the governor of the province ordered the tree-felling to stop and suspended the eucalyptus planting project.

Suspicion and distrust, however, linger on as the villagers carefully watch officials' moves so they can prevent their forest from being invaded again.

much the forest matters to us."

Villagers had swallowed their resentment as they watched strangers intrude upon their land to destroy their ancestors' property as if they, the villagers, did not exist.

Poh Siri says he fell sick from the pain and anger. He was unable to sleep for days after the tractors crawled onto their land and began felling the forest.

"But then I decided to fight. We had to unite and plan our strategy against this. We could not let our forest disappear before our eyes and do nothing to stop it. The moment I made up my mind to act, all my sickness disappeared."

For as long as anyone can remember, the 1,000 *rai* of natural forest has served as a vital source of food and firewood, while parts of it have been used as grazing ground for cattle by more than ten surrounding villages.

"It has always been our forest, " says *Poh* Siri. "We have our own rules to protect it, to stop the villagers cutting the big trees down, to preserve them for our children. But one day, a wire fence was put up, and we were told that the forest was no longer ours. It seemed as if these outsiders could do anything they pleased with it. We couldn't allow that."

"Why cut down trees to plant trees? Why destroy an important source of food and medicine?"

▼ Forest trees at
Nam Kham

Huge, sky-piercing trees stand majestically in the thick forest of Nam Kham. The 50 *rai* of land left bare as a result of the destruction by the tractors two years ago provide a sad contrast to them.

During the heated protest, the confrontation was intensified when villagers from the nearby Weeping Tungkula Plains came to offer support against the eucalyptus plantation.

"Officials had told them that the eucalyptus would help nourish their arid land," says *Poh* Siri. "But as it turned out, they could no longer use what had been their forest. The cows and buffaloes would not enter the plantation.

"They said it was really an eerie place - no grass, no other plants and the earth had become hard so quickly after the eucalyptus trees had been planted. No ants, no insects, no birds, no mushrooms, none of the things

that we're used to getting from our natural forest. We could not let this happen to us too."

No academic or scientific reports can convince the villagers to believe otherwise.

"We've been living closely with nature all our lives. We trust our own observation of the way nature has changed," says *Poh* Siri. "We've visited those other places which have been afflicted by these strange trees and seen for ourselves."

He says that villagers are in favour, however, of the reafforestation project. "But why only with eucalyptus?" he asks.

To show that they are not against this national reafforestation policy, the villagers have planted trees which give edible fruits such as tamarind and *keelek* in the vacant plot originally intended for the controversial eucalyptus.

"It is not true that the Isan soil is so infertile that no trees can grow except for this strange new plant. Just look around for yourself," says *Poh* Siri, pointing at the lush forest.

Although all is quiet on the official front concerning the suspended eucalyptus project, *Poh* Siri says his villagers are ever ready to respond to any suspicious move.

"We have no choice but to protect our land and forest. We are poor farmers, and we need the forest to give us food. But city people never seem to understand this. They're not used to hunger and poverty." ■

Protecting a community forest

Village headman Sawaeng Bootwong, aged 46, swears he and his villagers will follow in their fore fathers' footsteps to protect their 1,400 *rai* Nonlarn forest from destruction.

That includes burning down the forest concessioners' office, chopping down eucalyptus saplings and guarding their village with security as tight as if it were a war-zone.

The seemingly submissive, peace-loving Isan villagers turned into an angry mob when the company, which had won a concession from the Forestry Department to plant eucalyptus trees there, sent in bulldozers to level the forest greenery to make room for their commercial project.

"We were burning with anger and hatred, watching them destroy our forest," says Sawaeng. "Who do they think they are? Where do they think they come from? How come they have the right to trample on our property?"

The village headman's resentment is clear as he relives the scene in front of an area of rich forest, declared by Forestry Department officials as 'deteriorated' and therefore suitable for reafforestation.

It is an understatement to say that the villagers are unhappy with the Forestry Department's policy.

When the Department declared the area reserved forest in 1971, nine villages which had been living there for more than three generations effectively lost ownership of their homes and ricefields, and were considered intruders on their own land.

"It would have helped a lot if the officials had visited us first, asked us what the situation really was, and then classified the forest area in a realistic manner," says Sawaeng, insisting that the villagers were not informed of the demarcation of the reserved forest.

"And I still can't understand how on earth our forest could be considered as deteriorated," he complains, looking around at the cool greenery.

Besides lumber and forest products, Nonlarn is also an area rich in laterite. Villagers frequently express their resentment at seeing countless truckloads of coal rumbling past their houses.

"This is our forefathers' property, but we have no say in what can be done here, not to mention any chance to benefit from it," says Sawaeng .

Baan Siao in Si Sa Ket province is the oldest of several villages at the edge of the Nonlarn Forest and has the closest affinity with the community jungle.

Headman Sawaeng still remembers vividly how, when he was a child, his parents and other villagers who had encroached on the forest to plant jute and tapioca agreed to pull back and let the woodland recover from

"We are fighting for younger generations whose hunger can be eased by food from the forest."

▼ **A forest livelihood**

the damage caused by growing these cash crops.

"People thought they had to till more land to survive," he says. "But it turned out that the rains did not come as usual, and we suffered even more. So the villagers agreed to preserve the forest, and we've never had any serious droughts since."

Baan Siao shares the forest with other villages, but a journey through it shows marked differences. Because of *Baan* Siao's forest preservation policy, its side is still forested in contrast to the tapioca plantations on the other side.

Prizing themselves as protectors of the forest, the *Baan* Siao villagers' anger at the sight of the bulldozers rolling in is understandable. One day, men and women, young and old, marched along the winding, dusty road to the fenced-off forest, armed with knives and spades, and swept clean 200 *rai* of eucalyptus saplings in less than an hour.

Two days later, they burned down the office of the Forestry Department which had granted the concession to the company to plant eucalyptus.

Today, the area is full of shrubs and foliage which indicate the forest's fast recovery, despite officials' claims that the area is so infertile that it is suitable only for diehard varieties such as eucalyptus.

The villagers intend to press on with their struggle by petitioning their Members of Parliament, maintaining their show of unity, and backing up their claims with proper academic studies to show that theirs is a healthy, not deteriorated, forest, says the headman.

Although the Forestry Department and the concession company are retreating for the moment, the villagers are still worried because the 15-year concession contract is still legally effective.

For the protest leaders, however, the future of their forest is not the only concern. They also fear for their own safety.

"I have been offered bribes and been threatened when I turned them down," says Sawaeng, a father of five. "I admit that I'm afraid. But if we don't stand up to them, how can we hope for fair treatment? We are fighting for the villagers and for our younger generations whose hunger can be eased by food from the forest. We think it's something worth risking our lives for." ∎

Striking a spiritual balance

▼ *Luang Pob*
Khamkian
Suwanno

Abbot Khamkian Suwanno realised that rural people would never be able to free themselves from desire if they could not first free themselves from hunger.

So he left his peaceful mountaintop retreat, moved down to the nearby Tah Mafai Waan village in Chaiyaphum province, and set about developing the remote frontier settlement.

That was ten years ago. From an outlaw community, riven by feuding and fighting, the village now lives in comparative peace.

With leadership from Abbot Khamkian, a forest monk and dedicated meditation teacher, villagers benefit from a rice bank, a temple nursery, a village cooperative shop, a community fishpond and a conservation education programme for children. The Abbot has tried to endow them as well with spiritual immunity against the wave of materialism that comes with development.

"But I would not call my work successful yet," says the sturdy monk modestly with a kind smile. "We've only come to the point where the villagers at least understand what I'm saying about the importance of a proper lifestyle, free of vice and superstition, about cooperation, compassion, and contentment, and about the concept of merit-making.

"Merit-making is being good to others and making others happy. You don't have to make merit by giving alms to monks.

"We still have a lot more to do."

Clad in a dark saffron robe, the bespectacled monk looks much younger than his 54

"Merit-making is being good to others and making others happy."

▼ *Luang Poh*
Khamkian
Suwanno

"Buddhist monks cannot deny social responsibility."

years. Born to an Isan peasant family, he is used to hard work. His cracked feet and sturdy hands attest that he is still very much a man of action.

Despite being a revered *luang poh* or abbot, it is common to see him building shelters in the temple, clearing the rugged path at his forest monastery, or fetching water from the temple's pond.

"I suppose I'm basically a do-er at heart," he says. "If there is something that needs to be done, I go ahead and do it."

Monks, as he sees it, cannot deny social responsibility. "And we are also to blame if the villagers are trapped in indebtedness. It is our duty to show the way."

At first, he says, the villagers offered him 5,000 baht to leave his forest monastery, his retreat on the nearby mountain, to come and stay in the village, because it was difficult to find a monk willing to live in their outback community.

"I refused it, and that was why they began to trust me and to listen," he says

At the crack of dawn, villagers wake up to the abbot's sermon, telling them that being good fathers, mothers or children, and fulfilling their duties is tantamount to merit-making.

"I also don't preach heaven and hell. I talk about here and now, about how to make Tah Mafai Waan a peaceful place to live in.

Hell is here, if we are constantly quarrelling."

Seeing that the villagers had to travel a long distance over rugged ground to buy rice, he formed a communal rice bank. A nursery was set up at the temple when he saw that the children were dying from malaria after following their parents into the forest. The community cooperative was started to help villagers economise, but there is no place there for alcohol, cigarettes, addictive pain-killers or the food seasoning, monosodium glutamate.

The abbot thinks that the villagers have had a constant battle with poverty and hunger because they have followed the mainstream, greed-motivated economy.

"They destroyed the forest to get land to plant tapioca for sale, because it was quick money. They weren't interested in planting or growing what they could eat. When tapioca prices fell, they ended up in hunger and indebtedness.

"They didn't realise that it is not how much money we make that matters, but how much we save."

He includes that point in his sermon, day in, day out. "Repetition and continuity are essential to instil new awareness," he says.

So instead of concentrating on tapioca farming and having to buy all their food from outside the village, he has encouraged the villagers to grow their own vegetables, dig family fishponds and grow fruit trees to be

"It is not how much money we make that matters, but how much we save."

self-sufficient in food.

But mere words, no matter how right they might sound, did not convince the villagers to change their way of life.

"We have to show them concrete examples that work," says the dynamic monk. "Villagers can't afford to take risks, because failure means a loss of livelihood."

At his temples, both in Tah Mafai Waan village and at the forest monastery, the abbot himself grew mangoes, limes and other fruit trees to show the villagers what they could do.

Near his forest monastery, he gave a plot of land to one family to experiment in vegetable gardening without the use of chemical fertilisers or pesticides. It was a complete success.

To broaden the villagers' perspectives, he encouraged them to go on field study trips to other northeastern villages which had been successful in this kind of integrated farming.

"Villagers are realistic people. They have to see to believe. And when they do, they change of their own accord."

But all these development activities, he says, are just part of his duty to create a favourable atmosphere in which villagers can develop their spiritual awareness.

"My main job is to teach meditation, to offer a way to spiritual liberation. If there are obstacles to this, such as the villagers' poverty and indebtedness, compounded by their own greed, vices, superstitions and ignorance, then I have to help them overcome these problems first, so that I can accomplish what I set out to do."

His meditation technique aims at making meditators masters of their minds. By developing mindfulness of their each and every movement, practitioners learn, step-by-step, to be keen observers of their own thoughts. They should be able to achieve an awareness of the nature of their minds with their tricky mechanisms, and to learn how to cut the links that lead to desires, disappointments and suffering.

"Then we can maintain our inner stability, despite outer turbulence," says Abbot Khamkian.

He has often been asked to move to Bangkok to teach meditation to educated people who want to learn, instead of being isolated in the remote countryside.

"But I think differently. I think I should stay where my help is most needed," he explains simply.

So his forest monastery has become a spiritual refuge for young university students in search of inner peace and insights into the meaning of life, or merely a rest.

They learn to cope with dead silence, with the loss of a sense of time, with a complete absence of hurry or the excitement of something new. They are free to engage in the struggle to be at peace with themselves - which makes the authorities eye the abbot with suspicion.

"It's not new to me to be labelled as a communist monk," he says, dismissing the issue with his usual gentle smile.

"It's understandable, because what I am preaching is different from traditional folk understanding about Buddhism, such as about merit-making. My answer is to stay here, keep on working, and let people see, understand and judge for themselves."

Despite much progress at *Baan* Tah Mafai Waan, the fatherly abbot remains uncertain as to what is to come.

"It is not easy to tame one's greed," he says. "I don't think I have been successful, as things stand now. The battle is still on."

With electricity, he says, comes television, which, through its advertising and urban-based programmes, brings a fierce stream of temptations and raised aspirations that few villagers find themselves strong enough to resist.

"Things might change quickly from now on. I might not be able to help much, now that the temptations are so strong. But at least I can say one thing, I can save the forest."

He can say that indeed. Abbot Khamkian has successfully turned what was once dry land at the temple in Tah Mafai Waan into a cool, green glade where one can retreat to practise meditation in peace.

At his forest monastery, he has managed to preserve against encroachment nearly 600 *rai* of lush, green forest atop the mountain. It is now the only greenery visible amid vast tapioca fields that stretch as far as the eye can see.

The abbot's close affinity with nature and the forest is obvious as he walks through the woods, touching the leaves gently, knowing practically every plant by name and its medicinal value.

"Nature is our greatest teacher. Apart from the wood's mind-soothing peace, you can get the answers to life's problems by carefully observing nature, the inter-relatedness of all things, the harmony and balance. Nature teaches us the value of simplicity as well as the essence of life.

"That is why I treasure the forest so."

To protect his greatest teacher, the abbot is planning to send monks to stay deep in the forest, so that villagers will not dare to damage the sanctified area, declared a forest monastery.

"I am greatly concerned about the rapidly diminishing forest. That is another reason why I stay put," he says.

"Meditation puts our minds in order and brings peace. The forest can also free our minds, if we can see through to nature. There is still so much to do here." ∎

Malnourished boy grows up

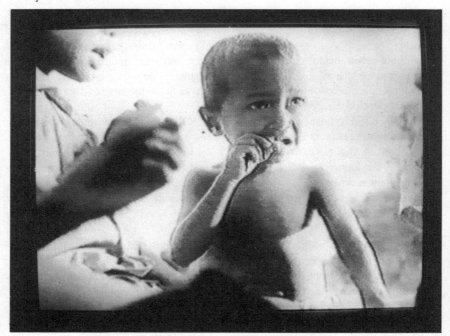

T he earth-eating boy, who shocked the Thai public two years ago into recognising the seriousness of child malnutrition in the country, is now a cheerful little kid.

Seven-year-old Boonruang Rayabsri is a far cry from what he was when the public saw him on television - a wrinkled young child who ate soil to ease his hunger, his empty eyes staring ahead hopelessly.

Boonruang, who is better known by his nickname, Noon, appeared as part of a campaign to create public awareness of child malnutrition. It stunned the nation. Noon became the focus of attention. And life has never been the same for him since.

"I now have lunch every day at school," reports the boy proudly with a big grin on his face. He hugs himself and smiles shyly when a teacher compliments him on his school

▼ Boonruang 'Noon'
Rayabrsi today

grades. In his Grade One class, Noon is second only to his friend, the *kamnan's* son.

The Foundation for Children's Development, which spearheaded the campaign, was subsequently able to sponsor a free lunch programme at the small village school in *Baan* Bor. Teachers say school attendance has consequently increased steadily and the children's health and learning ability have improved.

Once the very symbol of the malnourished child, Noon today represents an encouraging trend, showing the big difference public attention can make to hungry children in remote areas.

Although he is much smaller than most children of his age, Noon's skin no longer looks like fish-scales, and his brows are no longer closed together in constant frown, a sign of serious malnutrition.

▼ Noon and his
parents
▼ ▼ Noon's grand-
mother

But Noon's clothes are dirt-stained, and he walks to school barefoot. He still has to deal with never having enough school materials, such as books and pens. But that does not make him much different from many other school children. Now that his days of chronic malnutrition are behind him, he can laugh and play in the fields with other youngsters.

A small village of some thirty families in Si Sa Ket, one of the Northeast's poorest provinces, *Baan* Bor consists mostly of the Khmer-related, Suay ethnic group. Until recently, they lived in isolation with little interference from outside.

The village looks no different from most northeastern villages - a red dirt road, pervasive heat, thatched houses on high stilts - except that the

houses are smaller and much shabbier.

"I was born here," says Noon's 80-year-old grandmother, her ears adorned with earrings made from dried leaves according to Suay tradition. "I don't know how old the village is. But it has been here since my grandfathers' time."

Surrounded by vast ricefields, the village emerged from its obscurity when it became known nationwide as the village of the earth-eating children. It was her grandchild who made it so.

Although the publicity brought some positive changes to the village, feelings were hurt in the process. It was probably Noon's own parents who were most upset.

"I was angry. I was hurt," says 50-year-old farmer Chid Rayabsri of his

▼ Noon with school friends

feelings when he saw his son on television as the earth-eating boy. He sighs, looking uneasy and reluctant to talk about the incident.

His suspicion of outsiders is understandable. After Noon's television appearance, his thatched hut received visits from many strangers from the city who probed into his life, telling him what to do and scolding him for looking after his child so badly.

For the local authorities, the news of earth-eating children meant trouble as well -

and loss of face. Many did not hide their annoyance from Noon's parents.

Neighbours say Chid used to cry when drunk and express his anger against the accusing fingers which were pointed at him and his wife.

"Noon was born premature," he says, as he begins to look somewhat more relaxed. "My wife was almost fifty then. Noon is my youngest.

"Then there followed years of drought,

▼ **A free lunch
programme to
combat malnutrition**

alternating with flash
floods. Life was very
hard. But we did the
best we could." His
older children are all
grown-up and healthy.
There is a crack-
ling sound near the
shack. Noon's mother
is back from looking
for small shrimps and
fish in the swamp,
bringing home a bas-
ketful of clams for din-
ner. Her hair is
drenched, her old face
a map of the harsh Isan
life, her body skin and
bone.

"No, she doesn't
want to talk," explains
her husband apologetically. "She can't speak
Thai very well, so she feels embarrassed."

With better harvests at home and help
from outside, the children's health has improved remarkably, and teachers say there
are no earth-eating children left in the school.

Eating earth, says one, is an addiction
which is hard for the children to break.

"When they eat too much of it, the tissue
around their eyes turns yellowish and the
children become slow and lifeless."

To prevent the
children from eating
earth, the teachers
explain its health dan-
gers from the invisible
but harmful germs.
They use children's
friends as the teachers'
informants. But if the
carrot does not work,
the stick will not be
spared.

"It has been very
successful," say the
teachers.

But ask the child-
ren and you get a diff-
erent answer.

"We are not eat-
ing the earth because
we're hungry, but be-
cause it tastes nice," says a young orphan
who, so that she can have a regular lunch,
washes dishes for her aunt who sells food at
the school.

Another boy describes energetically the
different types of edible earth.

"This is *din jee*, the hard baked clay," he
says. "It smells very nice. The new and fresh
clay you find when you dig a pond is also
good. It's kind of sour. Ordinary clay is sort
of salty. And *din pluag*, the soft earth on old

▼ *Baan* **Bor children
with soft earth on
termite-eaten wood**

termite-eaten wood, is sweet and smells good."

He leads a bunch of friends off to nearby the school fence where the children make a dessert of *din pluag*.

"I don't think there's anything strange about eating earth," says one girl. "There is a big girl in our village who still eats it."

The elderly at *Baan* Bor insist, however, that it is a weird habit.

"It's like being addicted to smoking cigarettes," explains one. "You know it's bad, but you just can't give it up."

Freed from malnutrition, Noon does not have to worry about what the future might bring until five years from now when he finishes his compulsory education at the age of 12.

Many of the village children have left to work in the city as factory workers or as servants. Noon might soon be one of them - or maybe not.

"I want to be a farmer," he declares, again with his big grin.

Only time will tell. ■

A shining solution to poverty

◄ Kampa Tong-
ngern
▼ Sant Deesri

The youngsters are back. With them, they have brought urgently needed know-how. Life and hope have returned once again to the village of Don Han in Khon Kaen province.

Four years ago, there seemed no way out of the hand-to-mouth existence in which the villagers were trapped. Now, *Baan* Don Han is known in the area as a prosperous, gem-cutting village.

Instead of leaving home to work in Bangkok, young people from as far away as Phichit province, 250 kilometres to the west of Khon Kaen, come to this small village of 90 families to learn the precise craft, hoping that they too can go back and revive their stagnating communities.

The big change at *Baan* Don Han started when a group of teenagers, working in a Bangkok gem-cutting and polishing factory, decided to come home and set up their own business.

"We missed home so," says 19-year-old Sant Deesri, who looks like a Bangkok teenager in his trendy sunglasses, T-shirt and blue jeans. "No one wants to leave home and family if it's not necessary."

Apart from the pain of uprootedness and loneliness in the big city, the high cost of living there, which wolfed up most of their wages, also prompted the Don Han young people, who all worked in the same factory, to rethink.

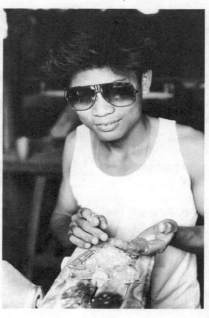

"We figured, why not use what we've learned in Bangkok to work at home? The earnings might be less, but we'll have fewer expenses as well," reasoned Sant. "The important thing is that the family will be back together again."

He and his friends wrote a letter home, asking for their parents' approval and support for their plans. A village council meeting was called and the proposal approved. To everybody's joy, the risk has paid off.

"I get more than I can earn as a maid in Bangkok and I don't have to put up with scoldings."

▼ **Gem-polishing at Don Han**

The airy spaces under the high-stilted, wooden houses have now been turned into small workshops where the youngsters work earnestly in the dim light, stereo music blasting away in the background as they transform lumps of artificial gemstone into sparkling, diamond-like dew drops.

"All the boys and girls have now returned home from Bangkok," says Sant's father and former village headman, Supat Deesri, grinning proudly. "No one wants to leave their families when there are jobs back here for them to do."

The trucks from a sugarcane plantation in the western province of Kanchanaburi came here last week and left empty, he says. "Only the stupid ones want to leave home now to be labourers."

At first, the village served as a home-based factory to supply the polished stones to the youngsters' old factory in Bangkok, whose owner comes from the village. Merchants in Khon Kaen province, however, saw promising business prospects, so set up shops to sell gem-cutting equipment and to buy the fin-ished products. With the market guaranteed, the business spread rapidly to other villages.

Baan Don Han now receives an endless stream of visitors from other villages which hope to duplicate its success. Some send their children to learn the skills, so they can return and add to their villages' income.

Kampa Tong-ngern, 13-years-old, is one of four young artisans from the lower northern province of Phichit who are learning gem-cutting at Sant's home factory. She gave Sant's family 700 baht for a three-month training course, including room and board. According to their agreement, she will get half of what she can produce in the fourth month and all of her production in the fifth.

"I now earn about twelve hundred baht a month. I only keep one hundred baht for myself and send the rest home," says the young girl proudly. "That's more than I can earn working as a maid in Bangkok, and besides, I don't have to put up with scoldings."

A strong sense of family responsibility is evident in both Kampa and Sant. What they earn, they say, is not personal but family

"We've got to combine industry with farming. We can't rely on the gem business alone."

▼ *Poh* **Supat**

income. As part of the family, their duty is to contribute to its well-being, so their money must go into the family coffers with no questions asked. That is until they have families of their own.

"I've got to help," says Kampa. "If I don't, my parents will have nothing to eat. My money makes all the difference."

Although the new cottage industry has brought the village back to life, village leader Supat looks at the changes with a sceptical eye.

"I see this industry as only supplementary. Our main profession is still rice farming," he says. "It's dangerous to give up rice farming altogether to cash in on this trade."

But *Poh* Rai Meekhao, aged 50, is one of the rising number of farmers who no longer care about producing their own food and concentrate only on the gem-cutting business.

He is also one of the farmers who buy vegetables from Supat in addition to buying rice from the market.

"They might earn more, but they have to buy more too," observes Supat. "The price of gems is going down. We've got to combine industry with farming. We really can't rely on the gem business alone."

Apart from rice farming, Supat and his wife have dug family fishponds, look after vegetable plots and breed pigs and chickens to make their family self-sufficient in food.

During the rice planting season, Sant puts away his blue jeans and sunglasses and, along with his brothers and sisters, returns to the ricefields.

"One good thing about coming home is that I can help my parents plant rice," he says. "When I was in Bangkok, I used to feel quite guilty that I left them to work alone in the fields. Besides, I was born a farmer."

He only returns to his gem-cutting desk after the rice harvest, while his older brother goes back to growing mushrooms in a hut which he learned how to set up and maintain in Bangkok.

"I'm happy to have enough to eat and to be able to live adequately," says father Supat. "I'm happy that our family can be together and work for our well-being."

For the first time in his life, he says, he finally feels that there is hope on the horizon.

"I also feel that I've regained my self-esteem," he says. "Before, I felt that I was a lousy father and provider. I could not hold my family together, my children had to leave home to work. Now we can all work together. Now I can feel good about myself." ■

Plunder of the South

MYANMAR
(BURMA)

Phetchaburi

Phrachuab Khiri Khan

Andaman
Sea

Gulf of
Thailand

Chumphon

Ranong

Surat Thani

Phangnga

Nakhon Si Thammarat

Krabi

Phuket

Trang

Phatthalung

Songkhla

Pattani

Satun

Langkawi Island

Yala

Narathiwat

SOUTH

Penang

MALAYSIA

0   50   150   km

Bangkok

Plunder of the South

T he South of Thailand is often considered the richest region of the country because of its abundant natural resources. It is typified by tropical islands, palm-fringed beaches, coral reefs and marine life. Its 16 provinces make up about 15 per cent of Thailand's land area, some 77,550 square kilometres.

The southern population of more than seven million people make up about 13 per cent of Thailand's total population. Most of Thailand's two million or more Muslims live in the South; in the five southernmost provinces bordering Malaysia, the majority are Muslim, not Buddhist as in the rest of the country.

The South receives the highest annual rainfall of any region in Thailand, a contributing factor to its being one of the most abundant agricultural areas. It is Thailand's major source of rubber, coconut, tin and palm oil. The South accounts for 85 per cent of the country's tin exports and for 95 per cent of rubber exports, making Thailand the third largest rubber exporter in the world.

Subsistence farmers in the South usually have a small ricefield where they grow rice for their own consumption, supplemented by growing rubber and fruit and by fishing. Because of the South's extensive coastline, many people are seafarers and fishers. About 66 per cent of Thailand's estimated one million people who depend on fishing for their livelihood live in the South.

But the region's exotic image of prosperity has eclipsed the growing plight of the small farmers, fisherfolk, mine workers and urban slum dwellers who rely on the land and seas for their living. Many of them are now struggling to survive at a marginal level. They are apprehensive about a further push towards industrialisation and export-driven activities in the region because they will continue to reduce their traditional livelihood and to cause ecological degradation.

Thailand is now one of the world's top ten exporters of fish and seafood, and the top fishery producer in southeast Asia. But the continual and often illegal activities of large fishing trawlers have swept the coastal seas clean of fish, leaving little or nothing for local fishermen.

Despite this, most fishing families want to stay close to the seas and water to continue their traditional way of life. Many of them borrow money from local fish traders or moneylenders to buy larger boats and more advanced fishing equipment, but debt and being tied to the middlemen is often the only result.

Pollution and deforestation have contributed to the declining numbers of coastal fish and marine life as well. Many factories which have sprung up in the South in the past five years or so, many of them connected with the fishing industry as canners or freezers of the fish and seafood for export, discharge untreated waste into the surrounding fields, water sources and seas.

The mangrove swamp forests are the natural habitat and breeding ground of the fish and marine life. The spindly mangrove trees, with their multi-branched visible roots growing in the muddy sands in a few inches of sea water, have been felled for timber and charcoal production and to make way for aquaculture, mainly prawn farms. Over half Thailand's mangrove forests have been destroyed in the past 20 years, the highest rate of loss in the past decade when the main cause has been the prawn farms.

Prawn farming started in the South over ten years ago, but has boomed in the past three years since farms in Taiwan became unviable after their five to ten year life. The area in the South given over to prawn farms more than doubled from 1977 to a 1987 level of 522 square kilometres, estimated to increase still further to some 800 square kilometres in 1989.

The black tiger prawns are raised in huge three acre ponds in a mixture of fresh and sea water, which is why the farms usually have to be within one to two kilometres from the sea. The bulk of this luxury seafood is exported to Japan.

Despite the current high returns, the capital investment needed in prawn farming - for canals or pipes to draw up the sea water, pumps to circulate oxygen in the ponds, electricity to drive the pumps, refrigeration equipment and to dig the ponds - is too high for most small farmers and fishing communities.

Many of them have instead sold their coastal land to domestic and foreign prawn farming companies at high prices, paid off their debts or bought consumer goods, but lost the source of their livelihood in the process.

Negative ecologcial effects have already been observed in some areas, such as a shortage of underground fresh water, and the seepage of salt water from the ponds into surrounding ricefields, ruining the soil and crops.

The southern hills and mountains used to be covered with tropical rain forest and rubber forests in which rubber trees were grown alongside fruit trees and other plants, giving food and forage to local people. But rubber trees of a high-yield variety have almost completely replaced them since government promotion of rubber for export started in 1961.

The destructive flooding and landslides in the South in November 1988 were attributed to this loss of the natural forest and prompted the government to ban logging nationwide and renew its efforts to reforest the country. Changed and unpredictable weather patterns are also attributed to the loss.

The rubber plantations provide work for local people, although they often receive less than the minimum wage. Many villagers grow small amounts of rubber themselves, but need at least 14 *rai* to make ends meet.

The sun and sand of the southern beaches and islands make the South a popular international tourist destination. Tourism is now considered Thailand's top foreign exchange earner, generating over three billion US dollars in 1988 and drawing nearly five million visitors in 1989.

But besides environmental damage from the unchecked growth of hotels and resorts, including erosion of the beaches and pollution from untreated waste poured straight into the sea, the loss of land and way of life is the major adverse effect on local people, especially those who need access to the beaches and seas to make a living.

All these difficulties in the countryside are pushing people off the land into the towns where they face hardships common to many slum communities - a lack of basic amenities, such as water and sanitation, eviction threats, insecure low-paid work and narcotic drug use.

Thanks are due to the following organisations for their assistance with *Plunder of the South:*
  Fishing Community Integrated Development Project, Songkhla
  Foundation for Human Settlement, Songkhla
  NGO Coordinating Committee on Rural Development/South
  Raindrop Association, Trang
  Small Rubber-Growing Communities Development Project, Satun

Plunder of the South was first printed in the *Bangkok Post* in May 1989

Tourism in, fishermen out

The sandy beach and turquoise-blue sea are now too good for a simple fisherman like Mala Kasim.

Last month, he had to move his small shack on the seashore to the rim of the mangrove forest deeper inland. Two of his neighbours have just joined him. More are expected.

"We have nowhere else to go," says Mala's daughter, while her parents are out at sea in their small boat. They have left their children to take care of the house, a hot and stuffy one-room shack which houses seven people. The sea breeze, blocked by the mangroves, is now a luxury for Mala and his family.

Land eviction is a new problem at *Kob* Muk, a peaceful island only 30 minutes by boat from the Haad Chao Mai national park in Trang province. Over the past three years, the tropical island has attracted land speculators from the towns in search of a purer holiday retreat. Once remote and of no commercial value, the palm-fringed beach is now worth its weight in gold as a potential tourist site. Power speaks. Mala Kasim and other fishing families simply have to go.

"I've lived here since I was born," says Jato Jiayan, a lively, elderly, Muslim widow. Her thatched hut is the first one along the sharp edge of this long stretch of the island, which is populated by some 200 families, mostly Muslims.

"This is a very good island," says the old woman, busy cleaning a small fish and paying no attention to her forefinger which is swollen from a knife wound.

"Here, even an old woman like me has enough to eat. I can fish near the beach. I can pick up the fallen fruits on the mountain. You don't have to be afraid of starving, even if you don't have a husband to take care of you," she says, showing her betel-stained teeth as she smiles.

But like Mala, Granny Jato has to leave. "There is no choice," her voice drops, followed by a deep sigh. "They say it's their land. They say they bought it from the land officials in the city. Although we live here, we don't have the money to buy it."

Her family has lived on the island for as long as she can remember, but Granny Jato says they never thought about land ownership.

"We just could not compete with the big money and modern equipment of the trawlers."

▼ Jato Jiayan

"We stay where there are fish and where we can keep our boats from the storms. If things are not good, we just move to a new place. The sea is our livelihood, not the land."

A group of fishermen are gathering nearby under the shade of the coconut trees. The gentle breeze and soothing sound of the wind-ruffled palm leaves belie their troubled minds. A few forlorn, thatched huts stand close by, half-torn down, testifying to their worries.

"We never thought we'd have problems like this," says Tam Sae-ngao, aged 43.

Tam's skin has turned brown in over 30 years of being exposed to winds and seas on *Koh* Muk. His more frequent contacts with the outside world and higher education have made him more articulate than most of the normally submissive Muslim fishermen.

"Before, nobody was interested in the land. We were free to build our houses wherever we wanted near the sea, as long as the land wasn't occupied. Our problems were at sea, fighting the big fishing trawlers," he says.

Land eviction is only the latest of several problems that have come to the island as the cash economy and modern technology have rendered it more accessible.

The first big problem was the modern trawlers.

"They use very fine nets, those damn boats," says Tam. "They have swept off most of the fish along the coast.

"They often sweep away our crab traps as well, so we have to borrow more money to make new traps. They've made our life so hard."

Like the inhabitants of many fishing villages along the southern coasts, the *Koh* Muk fishermen quit fishing more than 20 years ago, turning instead to crabbing and squid fishing, because of the trawlers.

"We just could not compete with their big money and modern equipment. Ours are only small boats with small engines," explains Tam.

To survive, many fishermen sent their young boys to work for the trawlers.

"I want to fight. But most Muslim villagers don't want to. They're peace-loving people."

▼ A small fishing
boat left ashore

"We're lucky now if they don't come back drug addicts," says Tam of the narcotic drug problem, rampant in almost all southern fishing villages.

As life became more difficult, many fishermen left the island to find other jobs in the nearby big town, mainly in frozen seafood factories, a booming export business, or in restaurants.

"We don't want to leave. This is the only way of life we know," says Tam. "But we have little choice.

"I want to fight," he says. "But most Muslim villagers don't want to. They are peace-loving people who don't want to be bothered," he sighs with frustration.

Some may call it submissiveness, but to the Muslim fishermen, it is sheer pragmatism.

"These outsiders have money and power. They can have us shot down anytime and no one will make amends," says one elderly villager.

According to the villagers, *Koh* Muk has been populated by Muslim fishermen for

▼ *Bung* **Suwit**
   Tongchoo

more than 200 years, as testified by the village cemetery. The Chinese moved in later from Penang in Malaysia to invest in the fishing business.

With their urban backgrounds, the newcomers obtained legal rights over the land and passed them on to their descendants. But when the land still had no value, life went on as it had for centuries for the Muslim fishermen. That is, until a few years ago when tourism reached Trang, one of the few places in the South which still had a beautiful, natural environment.

Most fishermen, however, don't blame the landowners. "I would have sold the land too. The city people offer so much money," says one.

Sitting close by is *Bung* Suwit Tongchoo, a quiet Muslim fisherman whose hair is matted together with salt from dried sea water and whose face is drenched with the sun. He puffs away at a cigarette, made from a dried leaf rolled around finely-chopped tobacco, listening with a dead-pan expression on his face to his neighbour talking about the problems, as if they had no bearing on his life.

Resigned to the conflicts, *Bung* Suwit will soon join Mala and the other fishermen who have moved inland to the mangrove forests.

"We can no longer nudge in between our neighbours' houses like we used to. Now that land has a price, everybody is worried that others may intrude on theirs," explains Tam for his quiet friend.

Moving inland makes things difficult for a fisherman who has to keep a constant watch on his boat, the main tool of his trade.

Like Mala Kasim and other villagers now living in the mangrove forest, Suwit will have to walk a long distance from his new home to the shore in the middle of the night to move his boat with the tide. If they are left ashore, the boats are bound to be stolen.

Tam sighs while his quiet friend stares out at the sea. "Life will no longer be as simple as it was before," he says. ∎

Fighting a no-win battle

▼ Yapa Kingkohyao

Yapa Kingkohyao had the shock of his life last year. When he went to pay his annual land tax, he found that the land was no longer his.

"But I didn't dare protest," he says. "I'm just a small peasant."

His land was a small plot of rubber on a hillside for which, he says, he has paid regular taxes for the right to till it.

The source of his livelihood is now in the name of an influential person from the town, someone certainly capable of flexing muscles stronger than Yapa's when it comes to dealing with officials on the issue of encroachment.

To make matters worse, his small ricefield is also threatened with confiscation. Like his rubber plot, his ricefield is in one of Trang's most scenic areas, Haad Chao Mai, which was

▼ **Fishing for a livelihood**

recently declared a national park.

"I feel robbed," says the peasant. "We've been living here peacefully all our lives. The land had no value whatsoever then. There were only poor people like us living there in the wild."

Not anymore, though. The once-isolated area of *Baan* Changlang in Trang province is now easily accessible via a network of roads.

There are only a few forested areas left amid all the mountainous rubber and palm plantations, mostly owned by money-barons from the towns. With tourism booming and new cash crop plantation schemes, this coastal area has become prize property.

Pushed off his land, the once self-sufficient farmer now lives hand-to-mouth as a wage earner.

▼ Changlang
fishing village

"I have a small boat," says Yapa. "But I've been a farmer all my life. It's hard to learn to be a fisherman at my age."

Yapa looks much older than his 58 years, suggesting a ruined tree, stripped of its boughs after a heavy storm. His tall, weather-worn frame is starting to bend, his face is lined with deep wrinkles. His sturdy long arms and legs hang loosely from his body.

"When I found out that I had lost my land, I couldn't eat, I couldn't sleep. I have nothing left," sighs the old man deeply.

Yapa is in the same situation as hundreds of other villagers at *Baan* Changlang. Although the village has a 300 year history, its inhabitants were told to leave when the area was turned into a national park. Villagers are not legally allowed to live in national parks

"We are just proxies in this war. No matter who wins, we lose."

▼ **Changlang
fishing village**

or reserved forest areas.

They feel, however, that they are being hustled out of the way in the land controversy which involves forestry officials, money barons and themselves, the indigenous Muslim fishermen.

"We are just proxies in this war," says one villager. "No matter who wins, we lose."

Like Yapa, many villagers have found that strangers with money have quietly acquired rights over their land from the

local government Land Department, even though it is in a reserved forest area.

Meanwhile, speculators are eyeing the golden beaches and blue seas of Haad Chao Mai as a potential, money-making, holiday haven. They are lobbying hard to turn the national park into a resort to follow Thailand's well-known resorts of Pattaya and Phuket.

Villagers say the speculators from the towns have teamed up with local influential people and forced the villagers to sign

"With the authorities, at least there are some rules. With the money barons, bullets are the rules."

petitions, demanding that the beach be run by the provincial authority, so that it can be developed into a holiday resort.

"Who dares to say no, with their money and guns?" they say. "We are just being used and cannot say a word, even when we know that, if the demands are met, we will certainly be evicted, one way or another."

Compared with struggling with Forestry Department officials over confiscation and eviction from their land in the national park, the villagers agree that it is a whole different game fighting the money-barons.

"With the authorities, at least there are some rules. With the money-barons, bullets are the rules."

Despite *Baan* Changlang's long history, very few villagers have legal rights over their land, which puts them in an extremely vulnerable position in any legal controversies.

The idea of land ownership is totally alien to many villagers.

"It is simply not part of our tradition," explains one elderly villager. "In the old days, we shared everything, even our rice, because we are all kin. The village barn was under the *tonglang* tree. That's where the name of our village comes from - *chang* means barn and *lang* means tree."

For those in the village who are fishermen as well as farmers, their constant struggle with the uncertainty of the winds and seas made the idea of land ownership even more remote, he says.

One village leader says the lack of land documents has led to the villagers' being severely exploited by loan sharks. Their interest rate is as high as five per cent per month.

"Apart from eviction, indebtedness is our most urgent problem," he says. "Most of us have debts ranging from a few thousand baht to a few hundred thousand."

An attempt to compete with modern trawlers and a desire to "have what the city people have" are the two main reasons for their indebtedness, says the village head.

"Our traditional small boats without engines became obsolete when the trawlers came. We just had to adapt if we wanted to survive.

"And when the neighbours have televisions, refrigerators, motorcycles and pickup trucks, it's hard not to become envious and want them for yourself," he says.

Sitting nearby, old Yapa does not seem to hear his village head analyse the ills which have destroyed their once peaceful village.

Shoulders drooping, the old man still cannot get over his grief at his loss.

"They could have at least left me a few *rai*," he mutters to himself. "But they took them all. I can't understand it. I'm so poor and they're so rich." ■

Forests, fish, food - all gone

◀ Laem Makham

▼ *Toh Imam* Bu Nuansri and *Mah* Sani Nuansri

Natural abundance is a thing of the past in the Muslim fishing island village of Laem Makham in Trang province.

"In the old days, we didn't have to go far for fish, just wade in near the shore and you could catch more than enough to eat," recalls *Mah* Sani Nuansri, a 50-year-old, lively matron whose family has lived at Laem Makham for four generations.

But no one has done any fishing for more than ten years now. The trawlers, using very fine nets and explosives, have swept away the coastal fish, forcing the villagers to switch to crabbing and squid-catching.

"Our mangrove forest used to be so huge," she adds, extending her arms to stress her point. "And so tall! Your neck hurt to look up at the top."

But today, 40 years after the mangrove forest has been almost completely cut down to feed two charcoal factories in the village, the villagers consider themselves lucky if they find a piece of wood the size of their arm.

This island community is a 15 minute

"By the time we knew what was happening, it was too late."

▼ **Picking out finger-sized fish**

local villagers can do is look on at this new outrage to their land in silent bitterness.

Arriving at Laem Makham, it is not cool, fresh air that welcomes visitors, but the strong and pervasive aroma of burnt wood from the ever-hungry charcoal factories on the island, which some of the villagers work for.

"Our food has gone with our trees. Before, there were lots of crabs and fish in the mangrove forests. But they've all gone now," laments *Mah* Sani. "By the time we knew what was happening, it was too late."

Accustomed to abundance since childhood, she finds it hard to accept food scarcity as a new fact of life.

The matron sighs as she looks at dinner, one big, crispy, fried fish - and that a present from visitors - and a plate of her own finger-sized, fried fish. Small as they are, the fish bear deep slashes on both sides to cut the fine bones apart. Otherwise, they are inedible.

"In the past, when we found this kind of fish, we just threw them away without thinking," she recalls.

There is no squid or crab-meat for the meal, although the family, like most of the villagers, make their living from crab and squid catching.

"Those things hurt our stomachs - and our pockets," she explains, still able to laugh at the change in circumstances. "Simply too expensive for our tastes."

boat trip from the mainland, starting from a landing stage slightly inland at the edge of a waterway which flows out to the open sea. By the jetty is a charcoal factory which belches smoke, day and night, fed by piles of bone-like mangrove strewn in front of it.

As the waterway approaches the sea, the thin mangrove forest on both banks suddenly vanishes. The area has been cleared for profitable prawn farms which export the prawns they raise.

The project is illegal. But where money - and bullets - lay down the real law, all the

▼ Small fishing boats

But *Mah* still thinks herself lucky. At least she does not have to pay for the brownish rice, hot and fragrant on her plate.

"Of some ninety families in the village, only four, including us, have a small ricefield, so we don't have to buy rice. We are blessed," she says.

While *Mah* worries about the consequences of environmental degradation on her family's daily food, her husband, *Toh Imam* Bu, feels heavy hearted about its impact on his villagers. As religious and community leader, he says it hurts him to stand by helpless, watching the village slowly slip into bankruptcy.

Robbed of their livelihood by dynamite fishing and fine-net trawlers, nearly every family is now deep in debt, he says.

Dam Kekkerdpol, aged 38, pours out his anger against the trawlers. His crab and squid traps have been swept away by the trawlers twice in the past two weeks.

"I'm fed up with all this," he says "Seven hundred baht for a new one is a fortune for me. I will have to borrow money again from *nai pae*, the raft master. My debts are piling up. I just don't know what to do."

The *nai pae*, the raft master, is an integral part of southern fishing village life. He gives the villagers long-term credit for practically everything from fishing tools to seasoning powder. Their debts are paid off from their fishing catches at a price fixed by the raft master.

"We have no choice. We have no contacts outside to borrow money from anyone else," says Dam with resignation of the monopoly of the man he both fears and hates.

Fifty-eight-year-old *Imam* Bu says he has filed a petition with the authorities against the trawlers' violations of coastal fishing regulations, but to no avail.

"They told me that the trawlers pay taxes and we don't. The trawlers break the law by coming too close to the shore. But we end up in the wrong, not them. It's a farce."

Ethnic bitterness, initially hidden underneath social courtesy, finally slips out when emotions become too strong to suppress.

"It's as if they want to bully us Muslims," mutters *Mah* Sani, then politely retracts her comment.

Their resentment is understandable. On the other side are the trawlers, dynamite fishermen and greedy merchants who are Buddhist, a different faith from the fishing villagers. It seems they are all allowed to get away with anything by the authorities who are of the same faith as well.

The *Toh Imam*, however, has not lost his fighting spirit.

"If we can no longer find fish in the sea, we'll simply have to raise them ourselves," he says matter-of-factly.

Most of the villagers used to think fish-raising was only for someone as rich as the raft master.

"We thought that it would take as much as ten thousand baht to build one floating basket," recalls the *Toh Imam*, "which is obviously beyond our means."

But last year, he took a risk when the Raindrop Association, a local non-governmental development organisation, told him that a basket could be started for only a few thousand baht.

With encouragement and support from the Association, the *Imam* and a small group of villagers raised baby fish with left-overs instead of selling the small fish to the raft master as they usually did.

Their substantial gain at the end of the year dispelled all the other villagers' initial doubts.

"The villagers are not passive. They just cannot afford to take risks with something they are not sure of," explains the *Toh Imam*.

Most of the villagers in *Baan* Laem Makham now have their own small floating baskets. But the *Toh Imam* is still worried.

"They took our woods away, our fish as well. Now they pour poison into our canal. It's intolerable."

▼ **An island charcoal factory**

The poisonous water has killed the few remaining fish in the canal which is flanked by the ever-thinner mangrove forest.

"They took our woods away, our fish as well. Now they pour poison into our canal. It's intolerable," he frets.

The villagers are beginning to worry that the contaminated water will affect their fish-raising projects and dash their new hopes.

The old man's face drops as he thinks of his village's future.

"Our village is doomed," he says in a tone of grim finality.

"All our natural resources are gone - the fish, the food, the sea. No matter how hard we try, it seems as if we are hitting our heads against a brick wall.

"So far, we have been able to suppress our bitterness, because we believe that there will be a way out. But now, I don't see any, unless this destruction of the sea by outsiders is stopped quickly.

"We still keep our frustrations pent up. I'm really afraid of what will happen when they explode." ■

"Some of them have started to think too big," he says. "They borrow money to buy fish feed because they are trying to expand too quickly. They could easily get into debt if something went wrong.

"But they don't think. That's a sign of greed getting the upper hand."

His other worry is caused by the prawn farms in the cleared mangrove forests opposite the island, because they pose new threats to the village's livelihood.

The farms, he says, use poisonous chemicals to kill fish in the prawn nursery and then release the contaminated water into the canal which separates the island from the mainland.

When the resources run out

 ith the tin gone, the provincial town of Phangnga is almost deserted.

Once a centre of tin mining, it is now just a dreary spot to pass through on the way to more exciting places.

For 72-year-old Sa-an Dulayakasem, this atrophy is just another step in the decline he has seen since the collapse of the tin rush which powered the town for about 30 years.

They came, they saw, they conquered-

then the tin miners left just as quickly. But not before they had brought about a permanent change in Phangnga's landscape and its people's lives.

Beside the main road stands a run-down cinema. In front of it, a giant movie poster is now faded and torn. Strong gusts of wind whoosh through cracks and splits in the once-colourful images of stars.

The rest of the town is in no better condition.

▼ Sa-an
Dulayakasem

The small roads which connect the tin landings along the Klong Nag river with the main highway are lined with old, two storey buildings that look ready to collapse. Deserted, the meandering roads end abruptly in swampland covered by tall grass.

"There used to be a river over there," says Grandpa Sa-an. "But it's now very shallow because the silt from the tin mines filled it up.

"When I was young, there were ricefields along both banks. But when the river got so shallow, the farmers could no longer work on the land, so they left. I don't know where they went to."

Calm and accepting, there is no sadness in Sa-an's voice as he reminisces. "Things change. You can't stop that."

The changing face of his hometown is just part of the overall transformation of the South. The most obvious aspect of this is the imminent victory of the rubber plantations over the natural forest.

The green hills and valleys are covered with orderly rows of rubber, even though the land is not legally available for farming. Large areas of the plantations have been felled of trees. The land waits for new ones to be planted, so that from afar, the neat hills look like human heads with patches closely shaven by an electric clipper.

The rubber trees are the high-yield varieties, promoted by the national rubber organisation for export. Any weeds in between the rows of rubber trees are all removed, as they would gobble up costly chemical fertiliser.

Long gone is the era of the natural rubber forests, where the rubber trees were interspersed with a variety of indigenous trees and plants. Such forests were so thick that they served as giant parasols that let only a small amount of sun penetrate to the ground, and thus kept the air in the forest constantly moist and cool.

"I've seen all the changes in the way people think about rubber since it was first introduced in the South. First they resisted it, but things change and now it's the most popular cash crop," says Sa-an.

A second-generation Chinese, Sa-an's

"I think that it's the roads rather than the rubber trees which have swept the forests away."

▼ **Rubber plantation**

father was a contemporary of the nobleman Phya Rasadanupradit who introduced rubber trees into the South when it was covered with humid rain forests.

"Before that, people didn't like rubber trees because rubber is inedible and they didn't know where to sell the milk. Now, it's a different story. Now, we can even sell the bark."

But the change has taken its toll.

Sa-an says he suddenly realised that the singing of birds and the calling of gibbons had stopped. The frequent visits of wild boar and occasional ones of tigers, once part of his life, became things of the past.

"The changes were gradual. You didn't realise what was happening at the time. By the time you noticed, they were no more."

The muddy path for ox-drawn-carts, which once ran in front of his house, has long been replaced by a highway, with the roar of traffic replacing the sounds of the wild.

"I still think that it's the roads rather than the rubber trees which have swept the forests away," he comments.

Whatever the causes, the weather of late has been inconsistent, he observes. The rains come later and less frequently. For the first time in his life, he hears complaints of water shortages from people who are living in the mountains.

"The villagers say that they now have to dig ponds for water, because the mountain creeks have gone dry."

The old man blames these phenomena on the large-scale rubber plantations, mostly owned by money-barons living elsewhere who are eager to cash in on the expanding rubber export industry.

"Most simple farmers like us own only a small plot of rubber which we take care of ourselves. It's a way of life for us. For the rich, it is an industry, making use of cheap labour from the Northeast."

Massive encroachment on natural forest reserves perpetrated by these investors has caused the water shortage, he says.

"They are not planting rubber trees in the reserves little by little. Instead, they cut down the whole natural forest, thousands of *rai*, all at once.

"Then they burn off the undergrowth. The heat turns the topsoil into dry crumbs, which disappear and run off the slopes with the first rains. It takes four or five years for the rubber trees to grow big enough to provide shade for the ground. In the meantime, to make money, pineapples are planted between the rows of young rubber trees.

"In the years when the trees are maturing, there are no leaves to cover the earth to help retain its moisture. It's not surprising that, after the bare hills have been baked under the sun for years like that, the earth becomes dry and hard, no longer able to hold water."

Many people think that rubber plantations and natural forests are the same thing, since both are a mass of closely-growing trees. Grandpa Sa-an disagrees.

"You can feel the difference when you enter a natural forest.The air is moist, cool and much more refreshing, because of the diversity of trees and other plants. It is a source of food and medicine and a habitat of animals.

"You don't have any of these things when you grow only one type of tree in a rubber plantation and, worse still, cut them down regularly to plant new ones.

"But you don't have any choice, do you? The rubber plantation is the source of your daily cash, not the natural forest. You can't think too far ahead when it's a question of survival."

The climate has become irregular as well over the past 20 years, he observes.

"There are no distinct changes of season any more. There's no more winter. The cool breeze at the end of the year, which we call the kite-flying wind, has disappeared.

"There have been far fewer rainfalls. Before, it rained endlessly for months. I used to work as a labourer in a mine. During the rainy season, my hat would become green with moss because of so much rain.

"Now, we're lucky if it rains ten days in a row," says the old man.

"Because the changes in climate have been gradual, we don't feel it so much. It was different with the tin-mining industry. That was the heart of our economy. When it stopped, we were really hit bad."

Natural abundance is not the only thing that Phangnga has lost with its entry into the modern age. What Grandpa Sa-an misses most is not the greenery nor the predictability of weather.

"Our hometown is dry for lack of rain. But worse is the dryness of people's hearts," he says.

"Selfishness has replaced friendship and the sense of joy in sharing - those are the very precious things I miss the most." ∎

Crossing the border to work

Usen Tatoh has just returned to his village of Klong Song Pak in Satun province after a week of crab-catching near the Malaysian island of Langkawi.

He goes there every two weeks, leaving home with the high tides at the full moon and returning in the dark, star-lit night when the tide is at its lowest.

His 20-year-old daughter, Amsa, crosses the border too, but less often. Like the rest of the young women in the village, she goes to Malaysia twice a year to work as a wage earner in the ricefields, cashing in on the labour shortage there.

The able-bodied men in the village go as well. Their cheap labour is much in demand from those across the border who have been granted concessions to cut down the mangrove forest. Although the risk is high, so is the pay, which makes staying at home a senseless thing to do for those whose life is a struggle to keep ahead of bills and payments.

At *Baan* Klong Song Pak, there are times when the village of some 80 families is nearly empty.

"We have to cross the borders because it's no longer possible to make ends meet here."

▼ **Usen Taotoh, his wife and his daughter, Amsa Taotoh**

Seasonal migration across the Thai-Malaysian border to work illegally has been a way of survival for this Muslim fishing community for the past ten years since the thinning of the mangrove forests and the invasion of the trawlers, which have cleaned out the seas of the once-abundant fish, crabs and other edible marine life.

"In my parents' day, people didn't have to go very far from the coast. But things are different now, because there's less food and the number of people has grown," says Usen.

Sitting cross-legged in his simple wooden house, shaded by rubber trees, the turbaned elder explains the changes wrought in the village with graceful acceptance, if not resignation.

"You just have to take life as it comes and deal with it accordingly," he says quietly.

With a small ricefield, a rubber plantation and the abundant sea, Usen's family of eight used to be self-sufficient in food when the village was still isolated and they had little need of cash.

Expenses have since increased, many of them caused by the battle to cope with the competition of the trawlers for which Usen needed money for a small boat engine, gasoline and modern fishing tools.

In need of more cash and hoping to cash in on rubber's rising price, Usen decided to join the government's rubber standardisation

Apart from an ear-splitting chorus of cicadas which echoes throughout the small Muslim community, the village is almost lifeless. Empty houses line both sides of the dusty, orange road that leads to Usen's house.

"Migration is now a way of life here," says 58-year-old Usen, who is a *qateb*, the number two religious and village leader next to the *Imam*. "We have to cross the border to find work or food because it's no longer possible to make ends meet here."

▼ **Klong Sang Pak villager**

programme, geared towards exports. His traditional rubber forest was turned into a neat plantation of the new, high-yielding rubber trees. All the fruit trees in the traditional forest, which used to be another source of food for Usen, were felled, as required by the loan contract.

The old rubber trees gave much less sap than the new, high-yield variety, but were pest-resistant and did not need fertiliser. Usen says he sometimes feels doubtful of the returns when he now watches his hard-earned money disappear into buying expensive, chemical fertilisers.

It takes seven years for the rubber trees to become productive, so with pressing debts, Usen decided to risk venturing into illegal waters.

"I usually go with my wife in our small boat. Langkawi Island is not very far away.

"We all are afraid of being arrested. If that happens, our boat will be confiscated and we will be sent to jail. But we try our best not to cause problems. We are just small people trying to make a living."

His young and beautiful daughter, Amsa, full of hope, says she goes to Malaysia out of curiosity and a desire to be financially independent rather than from real need.

She says the village girls usually go in a big group after being contacted by middlemen.

"They pay for the transportation, border passes, everything. The work is hard, but we are treated very well, three meals a day with sweets in the afternoon."

She usually returns with pocket money of 2,000 baht after one month. "I never have that kind of money at home," she says.

Good money is the lure as well for the young men to cut wood for the Malaysian concessioners.

"I only have two small *rai* of rubber.

▼ **Southern Muslim
woman and
children**

"That's too little for us to live on," says Sit Sirsommart. "There's little risk involved in going to Malaysia. The *thao kae*, the wealthy Chinese entrepreneurs, have taken care of all that," he says.

He says the workers get paid according to the amount of wood they cut. "I can make up to one hundred baht a day," he says.

The wood cutters usually stay for several months. Their wives go along too with stocks of dry provisions to do the cooking because food is more expensive on the other side of the border. At night, they rest in simple shacks, covered with big plastic sheets to shield them from the rains.

With cash flowing in, new concrete houses are springing up back in the village, and there are growing numbers of television

▼ Klong Sang
Pak villager

sets, refrigerators and motorcycles.

But it has brought new problems as well. Addiction to stimulant drugs among young men is on the rise.

"The men take the stimulants so they can work at such a heavy job all day long, every day," explains Amsa. "Besides, the more trees they fell, the more they are paid."

Another village leader, Meed Ji-ae, aged 53, complains that community life is quickly breaking down because of the labour migration.

"Sometimes there are only a few old men left in the village. With nearly everybody gone, we cannot have meetings and put our heads together to develop our village as before. Nor can we have prayers together at the mosque.

"We are drifting off in all directions."

Meed also believes that the villagers' spending habits are corroding their values.

"We used to grow our own vegetables and catch our own fish. Now, everything has to be bought.

"The villagers buy without thinking. Pick-up trucks come to our village every day to sell cupboards, wall clocks, fancy pots and pans - all unnecessary things at skyhigh prices. But they still buy," he sighs.

As a carpenter, Meed is among the few who do not go to Malaysia to cash in on the higher wages there.

"It's too risky. The family is no longer a family. Besides, it's not how much money you've made that counts, but how much you've saved" he explains.

"I'm not in a position to talk, though. Even with scarce fish and low rubber prices, I can still earn a living as a carpenter.

"But it's different for the majority of the villagers. They can no longer depend on the sea, and their small plots of rubber are not enough to live on.

"They cannot stay on here. For them, there is no hope left in the village." ∎

Tourism means slum eviction

The fishing village of Kao Seng, jutting out of the long and sandy Samilah beach in Songkhla province, is being forced to move to give tourists another holiday spot.

Their homes of 30 years are an eyesore, in the eyes of the Songkhla provincial authority, so they have to go in the name of development.

"I've heard they are going to build hotels and things, like Phuket, perhaps," says Ji Wangnurak, a sinewy, 50-year-old fisherman. "We know it's good for the province, but it's a big blow for us.

"I don't want to go. But it seems that I have no choice," he says with anxiety.

Ji's hut houses two of his children's families as well as his own. Crowded in on all sides by other huts, it stands breathless by one of the sandy labyrinths which thread the little houses of the Kao Seng community together.

"It's a simple place, but it's good enough

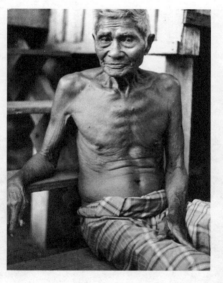

▼ A retired
fisherman of
Kao Seng

to live in. I can't afford to build a new house or to pay rent. It would take more than fifty thousand baht to build a simple house. I only have enough to live, day by day," he says.

Ji came to Kao Seng in 1957 with the first batch of fishermen from nearby Son On Jut. They were moved there by the provincial authority under the orders of the late strongman and prime minister Marshall Sarit Thanarat, who was reportedly displeased at the fishermen's poor sanitation.

The cause of the eviction has become a community legend. "He was really mad because he stepped on some excrement on the beach," says Ji.

Kao Seng, which was once a scenic spot with foothills and a waterway flowing into the sea, has been the fishermen's home ever since.

Since its beginnings as a small cluster of dwellings, the community has grown every year with the influx of bankrupt, landless peasants from the rural areas of the province

and subsistence fishermen from nearby coasts whose livelihood has been wrecked by the big trawlers.

Besides being subsistence fishermen and small vendors, the majority of the residents are wage earners who work for Chinese entrepreneurs, getting 30 baht a day for cleaning prawns, fish and squid which are dried for export.

Almost 80 per cent of Kao Seng residents earn less than 3,000 baht a month. About one-third of the slum dwellers are children. Although located in a municipal area, nearly 40 per cent still have to depend on underground water from wells rather than piped water. Toilets are the exception rather than the rule.

Poor sanitation and the smell from the dried, salted fish business have given Kao Seng a bad smell - and a bad name.

"They said our community troubles tourists because of its bad odours," says one villager sighing. "They said our houses are an eyesore, that we are ugly and dirty.

"Those who look down on us don't know what it's like to be poor and hungry."

▼ **The beach at Kao Seng**

"But those who look down on us don't know what it's like to be poor and hungry. If we could afford something better, we wouldn't want to stay here either."

To comfort themselves, the dwellers of Kao Seng treat the unsettling news of their eviction as mere rumour.

"No one has informed us directly about the eviction," says one community leader. "All we've heard is from news on the television. It's probably too much for those in power to lower themselves to talk to us."

The television news reported that they would be moved to another seaside location nearby where, only a few years ago, the Vietnamese 'boat people' who landed in Songkhla were put.

A slum dweller mocks this news. "It seems as if we're refugees in our own country," he says.

Ji looks at the situation more realistically. "They don't understand how we make a

"If we could afford something better, we wouldn't want to stay here either."

▼ Kao Seng fishing village

living. Us fishermen need a well-sheltered place to keep our boats, which the new place doesn't have. When a storm comes, our boats will be destroyed in flash.

"I wish they had asked us first, before they made their plans. Probably they think it's unimportant."

The residents are indignant at the announcement on the television that each family would be allotted a room of only five square metres.

"How can I squeeze my five children into such a small room?" asks one woman. "We all live in the same house, including my grown children. Am I simply to chase them away, just like that?"

The television report also included a promise that the Kao Seng dwellers would be allowed to live at the new place indefinitely.

"Words are just words. Our life has taught us that we cannot rely on anybody's words," says Ji.

"I can foresee more trouble coming for the poor. This is only the beginning."

▼ **Children of**
Kao Seng

After Sa-an Landing, Kao Seng is the target of the province's overall development plans to beautify the city to attract more visitors.

With a loan of 15 million baht from a foreign bank, the town of Songkhla plans to develop the seven kilometre beach from Son On Jut to the other end at Kao Seng.

In a spacious, air-conditioned room at City Hall, Mayor Prachote Ekuru talks of his beautiful dreams for Songkhla and Kao Seng.

"We are going to make Songkhla the centre of the fishing industry in the South. To do so, we need new ports to accommodate the growing industry. We must prepare ourselves for big changes."

Some 300 families at Sa-an Landing near Kao Seng have already been evicted to make way for the construction of a new port.

"I feel sorry for the people affected," says the Mayor. "But we have to consider the city's needs too."

"Kao Seng will be the most beautiful spot, just like it used to be before these people came," says Mayor Prachote. "We are just trying to save the place and give it back to the public."

He promises that there will be no construction of high-rise hotels on the beach. "That is, as long as I'm the mayor of Songkhla," he adds.

According to him, Songkhla is waking from a slumber to a bright future. Ji, the fisherman of Kao Seng, has something different to say. "I can foresee more trouble coming for the poor. This is only the beginning." ■

Pollution threatens farmers' livelihood

▼ **Polluted ricefields by a frozen seafood factory**

Villagers were delighted when a seafood export firm announced it would build a factory in Jana district of Songkhla province. They took it as a sign that progress was coming their way.

But progress has taught them a hard lesson. Many villagers now regret welcoming it without question.

In just one year since the plant opened, some 50 *rai* of ricefields next to it have become fouled. The cause is disputed. But it is clear to see that what was once paddy fields is now a stagnant, pungent-smelling swamp. The water is covered in places with a thick film of slime, infested with white worms.

A farmer cringes in disgust. "Look what they've done to our ricefields! To think this is only the beginning."

Farming in the polluted area is no longer possible. But farmers' problems do not end there. In the vast stretches of surrounding ricefields, the crop has not yet ripened,

"The more factories we have, the more our lives are intruded upon by outsiders."

food in and taking it out, frozen for export, mainly to Japan.

The back view of the factory, however, tells a different story.

Next to the back fence is a large pond, intended for the storage of waste water from the factory before it is treated. But the pond looks strangely beautiful, with blossoming red lotuses here and there. An open horizontal pipe sticks out over the water from one edge of the pond. It is supposed to carry polluted water from the factory. But not one drop emerges.

"Don't look there! Look here!" says a farmer, pointing at a ditch which runs past the edge of the pond and out of the factory grounds, carrying a steady flow of dirty water into the ricefields.

The farmers, who asked not to be named for fear of reprisals, a fact of life in the South, say they have complained to the provincial authorities, but to no avail.

"We were told to our faces that the factory was not the cause of the pollution in our fields," says one, "that the water from the ditch comes from the canteen and the living quarters of the factory's workers, not from the waste treatment system.

"Now we don't know who to turn to."

An elderly farmer whose ricefield has been polluted says selfish investment will erode the independence of villagers.

although harvest time is near. The ears of grain have not developed properly, say the farmers, who are worried that the crop will fail.

Seen from a distance, the factory stands between the polluted ricefields and a backdrop of deforested mountain slopes, partly covered by rows of rubber trees.

It provides more than 1,000 jobs for local residents and looks impressive, a collection of large buildings fronting the main road. Trucks come and go all day long, bringing fresh sea-

"We have to keep quiet, otherwise we will be kept quiet."

"Because of a scarcity of farmland in the South, us farmers only have small holdings on which to grow rice for our own consumption, not for sale.

"Of course, we're not as badly off as people in the Northeast. We won't starve if we don't grow rice, because some of us have orchards or rubber plantations to fall back on. But our lives will certainly be harder. It's simply not fair."

Sitting in the cool shade of a coconut grove, the old man sighs resignedly and slowly shakes his head.

"I've lived here for sixty years, since it was all jungle. Now we have roads, electricity, life is much more comfortable. But I'm not certain that all the changes are for the better.

"The more factories we have, the more our lives are intruded upon by outsiders. And the bitterest pill to swallow is the fact that the authorities won't give us a hearing."

The villagers say their ricefields are not the first to have been destroyed by untreated waste water.

"Not far away, thousands of *rai* at Nam Noi can no longer be farmed because of water pollution from a fish-canning factory. The fields are deserted. Our friends there have to buy rice - something their grandfathers never did.

"More and more factories are springing up in our district, so the problem is bound to get worse."

Rifts have arisen in the village between those whose ricefields have been affected by the factory and those whose children work there.

"It is difficult to organise ourselves to protest," says another farmer. "People who benefit from the factory couldn't care less if our ricefields are destroyed."

But there is disagreement even among those who are directly affected. Many of them think that to protest would be asking for trouble.

"They don't want to risk their lives. We know all too well that if anything should happen to us, the people responsible will not be arrested."

In such a situation, the villagers feel that they have no choice but to submit, although resentment of the officials and investors is growing stronger.

"We have no choice. We have to be quiet, otherwise we will be kept quiet," says one, glancing bitterly towards the factory.

"Having factories here is good because our children have to take jobs, since there is no more land left for them to till. If the factories are here, at least they don't have to leave home to look for work," he says.

"But if new jobs mean the loss of our old livelihood, then we don't think any of this is worth it." ■

Invasion of the North

MYANMAR
(BURMA)

LAOS

Chiang Rai

Bangkok

Mae Hong Son

Doi Suthep

Phayao

Chiang Mai

Doi Inthanon

Lamphun

Nan

River Ping

River Li

Lampang

Phrae

Uttaradit

Sukhothai

Tak

Phitsanulok

Khamphaeng
Phet

Phichit

Phetchabun

Nakhon Sawan

Uthai Thani

NORTH

0   50   150   km

Invasion of the North

T he northern region of Thailand is characterised by forested mountains and fertile river valleys. Bordered by Burma and Laos, it covers 100,000 square kilometres, most of which is mountainous or hilly, so that only about 10 per cent of the land can be used for lowland rice cultivation.

The higher land is used to grow fruit trees such as mango, lychee and longan, a small, dull, brownish-yellow round fruit on the outside but soft and sweet inside. Temperatures in winter are cool enough to permit cultivation of strawberries and peaches. The mountain slopes, which are reserved forest areas, have been used for small-scale cultivation of crops such as corn, ground nuts, beans, garlic, onions, cabbages and tobacco. A typical community in the upper North, located in the plains but surrounded by hills, may be involved in all these types of agriculture - rice, fruit and crop cultivation.

Of the upper-northern population of 5.2 million, over 80 per cent live in rural areas of which the vast majority are subsistence farmers. These include about 800,000 people of various minority ethnic groups, often called 'hilltribes' in Thailand, living on the hills and mountains.

Due to the fertility of the rice lands, a family owning about five *rai* of land can usually produce enough rice for its own consumption. This is between one-third and one-quarter of the land required by farmers in the more infertile Northeast.

Up until now, land has not particularly been a problem for subsistence farmers. But the growing population and influx of lowland Thais into the region, the full utilisation of the limited available rice lands, and widespread land speculation for tourist resorts and agro-industry mean that 45 per cent of farming families do not now have access to sufficient land to meet their needs. They survive by small-scale crop cultivation in reserved forest areas, illegal wood-cutting, charcoal production, rice-liquor distillation, working as daily hired hands when the opportunity arises, and by foraging for food in the forests - although it is becoming difficult for them to get by in these ways.

In Thailand's current economic boom, private companies are buying up fertile land for use as large-scale farms, fruit orchards, plantations and tourist resorts.

Other businesses are promoting wide-scale contract farming among rural communities. In the short-term, such schemes seem attractive and economically beneficial to rural farmers. Long-term affects are worrying, however, as the farmers become tied to and dependent on these agri-businesses with whom they have entered into a contract to grow crops.

Government and private-sector promotion of cash crops, which require a high investment, is decreasing the capabilities of small farmers for self-reliance and self-sufficiency in food. The increasing use of chemical pesticides is affecting the environment, soil and health of the farmers. As an alternative, some farmers are turning to integrated farming, which is based on principles of ecological balance and self-reliance, producing food for their own consumption before food for sale.

For those who do not have access to land, raising cattle is seen as the most promising means of long-term livelihood, because it requires little land or cash investment, only time and care of the animals.

Rural communities of the North have traditionally been fairly cohesive entities with strong cultural roots, independent community organisations, respected natural leaders and production methods based on mutual cooperation. Villagers worked together at rice planting and harvesting, and house building, and organised weddings and funerals together.

These traditional features have become somewhat diluted as the villagers are engulfed by the market economy, land speculation and tourism. Rural communities are gradually losing their unique cultural heritages and their sense of identity. Families are split-up with the youth leaving home at an early age. Evenings are spent watching urban, middle-class television soap operas which replace informal gatherings to discuss village affairs.

About 50 per cent of the North is now covered with trees, both natural forest and planted trees, compared with almost 70 per cent three decades ago. The rapid deterioration of forest areas, mainly due to legal and illegal, large-scale, logging operations, has badly affected water resources. Streams which used to run throughout the year are now dry for most of the time. Rainfall has decreased and become erratic. These changes have affected agriculture, while villagers living around forest areas find it harder to obtain food by foraging.

Northern communities face increasing debt problems because of decreased self-sufficiency, medical bills, consumerism and investment in modernised agriculture, such as mechanised ploughs, water pumps and fertilisers.

The debts can only be paid off by sending the youth to work in the cities, the young men as hired labourers or construction workers, the women as household servants or prostitutes. Prostitution is a common occupation among young women from certain areas of the North. It has become a major source of income and the 'key to survival' in the modern era.

Another motivating factor behind labour migration is the increasing need or desire for money. Rural people have developed a high demand for motorcycles, consumer appliances such as televisions and refrigerators, and other consumer goods. The rapid spread of good roads and electricity throughout the region has brought city life and consumer culture, continuously promoted through the mass media, into their homes. As agricultural income alone is not sufficient to buy these goods, the village youth leave for the cities to look for extra earnings.

The ethnic minorities living in the hills are subject to rigid controls, discrimination and exploitation. They are generally the worst-off of the northern population. They lack land and nationality rights and receive inadequate health and educational services. They are subject to forced resettlement and are often blamed for deforestation. Many of them have become popular tourist attractions.

As some hill people grow opium poppies for their own use and increasingly for sale to the heroin trade, they have been the target of crop substitution programmes.

Thanks are due to the following organisations for their assistance with *Invasion of the North:*
    Community Action Research for Development, Chiang Mai
    Community Culture for Development, Chiang Rai
    Dhammanat Foundation, Chiang Mai
    Foundation for Education for Development in Rural Areas, Chiang Mai
    Highland Community Ecological Development, Chiang Mai
    Mae-ow Project, Lamphun
    Northern Development Workers' Association, Chiang Mai
    Phayao Development Project, Phayao
    Project on Community Ecology, Chiang Rai
    Project for Ecological Recovery/North
    Sankamphaeng Rural Development Project, Chiang Mai
    YMCA Study for Rural Development Project, Lamphun

Invasion of the North was first printed in the *Bangkok Post* in January-February 1990

Under the speculator's hammer

Villagers in Pa Sang district of Lamphun province are fighting a new form of invasion.Hundreds of years ago, it was soldiers from neighbouring kingdoms and lands they had to struggle against.

Now, within less than two years, it is land speculators who have all but swept clean the villagers' community woods in their grand designs to turn them into plantations and resort homes for the city rich.

"They're not buying our land. They're stealing it and chasing us away," says farmer Sriyoon Suyapan of *Baan* Huay Pan Joy angrily.

His anger is shared by people in five other villages in the district where more than 10,000 *rai* of deteriorated forest have been taken over by the modern-day invaders.

While outsiders tend to think that farmers are striking it rich in the land boom in the North, the Pah Sang phenomenon tells.a completely different story.

"Big projects for plantations or resorts need huge areas of land. Our fragmented ricefields won't do, so they take our common woods, and we're robbed," says *Ai* Sriyoon bitterly. "That's what's happening in our vil-

lages and we are not the only ones, I'm sure."

Thousands of farmer families in the villages of Huay Pan Joy, Ton Kueng, Hua Huay and San Muang were dependent on the 10,000 *rai* of Pae Huay Kah woods as grazing land for their cattle and as a source of firewood, miscellaneous farm materials and food such as mushrooms, bamboo shoots and other wild vegetables.

There were no demarcation lines in the woods, but each village knew where its territory of more than 2,000 *rai* ended and another began.

Now only a few hundred *rai* of their woods are left, which villagers are urging the authorities to declare officially as community land to keep it out of the speculators' clutches.

"If we don't do something now, it will be too late," says *Ai* Sriyoon, an outspoken man in his 30s.

At any other time, *Ai* Sriyoon might have been just another face in the village crowd. He has not the land, the money, the age nor the education to make people listen.

But in this time of crisis,his articulateness, cynicism and daring to challenge the establishment have made him stand out as a

"They're not buying our land, they're stealing it."

▼ **Huay Pan Joy villager**

metres from the town of Chiang Mai, has only a limited area of farmland, like most mountain-embraced northern villages. Only one-third of the villagers are lucky enough to own a small piece of land which must be used extensively throughout the year, growing cash crops as well as rice, to make ends meet.

"But crop prices are so low. Garlic prices, for example, have fallen for ten years in a row. No matter how many additional cash crops we grow and how hard we work, we can hardly make any money. That's why we have to turn to the bank for loans," complains *Ai* Sriyoon about the nagging problems of cash crop prices and debt.

natural leader.

Ai Sriyoon and other Pah Sang farmers have learned a painful lesson about the inadvisability of leaving matters in the hands of village elders.

"Outsiders may have money, but they don't know which land is unused or is public land. But village heads and *kamnan*, the sub-district heads, know this in detail. Without local help, outsiders couldn't have swept into our land so fast," he says.

Ai Sriyoon's village, Huay Pan Joy, a big community of 400 families, some 100 kilo-

"We have to work as wage earners to supplement our income. And since many of us do not have land, we turn to cattle raising, which makes the common woods all the more important to our livelihood, because the cattle graze there."

But by the time the villagers realised the significance of their woods, it was almost too late.

"Because of poor soil quality and lack of water, few of us bothered to till the land in the woods which is the way to claim land ownership. And land had no value then, anyway.

"Those who did bother could only till

"We can no longer afford to be easy-going."

▼ **Cattle raising**

only a small plot of land, because they depended solely on their own labour," explains Chob Parami, a farmer in his 50s. "They could not afford to hire others to help."

A large chunk of the Huay Pan Joy common woods, about 600 *rai*, was sold to a big company years back with help from village leaders without any legal problems, although it involved the selling of public, not private, land.

The villagers, knowing better, kept quiet, thinking it was none of their business. Only recently did they realise that the fire had reached their front door when a land broker arrived with a photocopy of a land document to check the whereabouts of the area which had been sold. It turned out to be the remaining village woods, plus some 200 *rai* of land that villagers had claimed ownership of.

Ironically, the land broker's arrival

▼ **Farmers' tools hang
on a leaf wall**

occurred at the time when Huay Pan Joy villagers were starting to talk about having their remaining woods officially declared public property.

"It was the last straw," says Ai Sriyoon, who likens the land-buying boom to a raging typhoon.

"After sweeping through the surrounding villages, it hit ours about a year ago. Strangers would come knocking at our doors practically every day to buy, buy and buy.

"They wanted to buy our farmland. They wanted to buy longan orchards, but we don't have those any more because most of them were sold to outsiders a long time ago.

"These people! Why do they want to buy so much? Why don't they stop to think for a minute that they cannot take anything with them when they die?"

Despite his determination, Ai Sriyoon cannot help feeling paralysed in the fierce flurry of speculatory land purchases.

Only five kilometres away, more than 10,000 rai of common grassland in the village of Tah Loob are being turned into a huge estate of second homes in the country for town people. Young trees and bushes have been torn out of the ground. Tractors are busily paving a gridwork of roads among the small plots.

With the help of money's magic wand, the barren land will soon become a town-dweller's paradise, surrounded by green longan trees, set with a silvery, man-made lake, the River Ping flowing to one side of the estate and the famous Doi Inthanon mountain as a backdrop.

The villagers received about 600 baht per rai for the handful of land plots they had tilled and laid claim to. The same plots, when developed, are returning more than one million baht to their current owner - a simple reason why land speculation is spreading like

▼ Food from the woods

Close by at *Baan* Lao Pong Sua, a village of 200 families, the villagers do not know how many times their woods have changed hands since the old village head sold most of the land to sugarcane plantation owners about ten years ago.

And at nearby Hua Huay, the village of cattle herders has lost nearly 2,000 *rai* of its woods through an old trick that has never failed to work.

Land speculators bought up parcels of land scattered about the *Baan* Hua Huay village common by money-dumping and fencing-in. Then they sent in bulldozers to clear the fields and take over the whole area.

"I'm so angry," says *Ai* Sriyoon. "Local government officials are also making money as brokers. Instead of encouraging us to keep the common land, they told us to sell it, saying that our barren land would be developed and so bring in jobs for us.

"Land speculators have money. They

wildfire throughout the district.

At the adjacent San Mung village, more than 2,500 *rai* of their common woods have been fenced off by a Member of Parliament who now rents the land from the local authorities.

"The better educated they are, the better they know how to rob us."

have connections. Any legal documents they need, they can just get them made. They offer us only dreams to get out of our rut. We're fighting a losing battle."

Since the common woods have now nearly all been taken over, but the promises of jobs never fulfilled, the villagers are forced to fight back.

Blessed with a kindly climate, natural abundance and a rich culture, northerners have long been thought of as the most easy-going people in the country, conciliatory to the point of being submissive.

"We can no longer afford to be like that," says Sriyoon. "This is a matter of life and death."

At *Baan* Hua Huay, the villagers have taken action by petitioning the district forestry office to recognise the remaining 500 *rai* of public land as community woods before they are gobbled up by outsiders.

Baan Hua Huay is a small settlement of about 40 families. Most of them are landless farmers who settled on the fringe of the woods to raise cattle for rich farmers, in return for which they keep half of the calves born.

Villagers at *Baan* Lao Pong Sua are also petitioning the district forestry office to ensure that the rest of their woods do not change hands.

Ironically, they are waiting endlessly for official approval of their ownership of the woods which have actually been theirs for

centuries, before the advent of political centralisation.

At *Baan* Huay Pan Joy, however, villagers have to overcome the legal stumbling block of double land documents before they can follow the example of neighbouring villages in setting up official community woods.

Like other village leaders fighting for community forest elsewhere in Thailand, *Ai* Sriyoon and his friends have learned fast that they are risking their necks in fighting big money.

"We don't have any choice," says *Ai* Sriyoon. "It's hard fighting educated people. The better educated they are, the better they know how to rob us."

Baan Huay Pan Joy villagers often call their fields the Crying Land.

"We work the fields to death all year round. The land has no time to rest," explains Sriyoon.

But if land speculation goes on unabated, there will be a new explanation.

"Old owners will be edged out. The land will no longer hear the language that has been used since the time of our ancestors. It won't be able to understand the words of the city invaders.

"People will still call our home village the Crying Land, because the land and the farmers have been parted." ∎

Youngsters fight for land rights

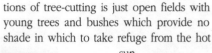

By tradition, the elders hold the reins of village politics. But the young people at *Baan* Nong Khiad in Lamphun province have decided that they no longer want to put up with that.

"The elders have all been bought off by land speculators. We can no longer trust them," says Witaya Manotham, a fiery young man. "Our livelihood is at stake. No elder in authority cares to look after our interests. That's why the young people have to come together to fight."

Witaya is one of a group of mostly young men in their early 20s who are fighting to save their village common from being taken over by a dairy company.

Although the villagers still call the common the forest, what remains after genera- tions of tree-cutting is just open fields with young trees and bushes which provide no shade in which to take refuge from the hot sun.

"To outsiders, this may seem to be just a wasteland lying pitifully idle. With their money, they think they can turn it into some- thing useful. But for whom? Certainly not for us," says Witaya.

Blessed with the cool shade of longan fruit trees, the mind-soothing greenery at *Baan* Nong Khiad itself belies the tension, anxiety and enmity that has been hov- ering over the vill- age for two years.

The villagers are locked in con- flict with the dairy farm company, which has already taken over the common grassland in the next village and is trying to extend its territory into *Baan* Nong Khiad.

"If the rich take the grassland away, it's the end of me."

▼ Cattle herding

The conflict started when, out of the blue, a convoy of bulldozers rolled onto the common to flatten the bushes and trees and turn the parched land upside down.

"The deal was made without any of us knowing. The brokers contacted the *kamnan*, the sub-district head, who contacted our village head. They worked as a team, at our expense," recalls 32-year-old Nop Foodontong, a rice farmer and cattle herder, hatred sounding in his voice.

But the villagers, he says, rushed in droves to stop the bulldozers in a tense confrontation that almost saw blood spilt. Eight in ten of the village's 165 families are landless and depend on the common grassland to graze cattle.

"Most of the longan trees you see around here are not ours," explains *Ai* Nop. "They were bought by outsiders a long time ago. We only take care of the orchards and receive ten

"If we don't do anything, no one will."

▼ **Nong Khiad**
   farmer

per cent of the yield," he says.

For a 56-year-old landless peasant like Tong Mahyong, cattle herding is the only way to make a living.

"It doesn't need any investment. We take care of the rich farmers' cattle and get half of the calves born in return," says the worn and weathered peasant, coughing. "It means an old man like me can still work, because cattle herding doesn't need much labour. All I need is time and grass. If the rich take the grassland away, it's the end of me."

With the village elders siding with the money barons and betraying their traditional duty as dependable patrons in a time of crisis, the young men felt they had the right to take matters into their own hands.

The support they have received from most of the villagers has made them feel confident to handle any opposition from relatives of the village leaders.

"If we don't do anything, no one will," explains Witaya matter-of-factly. "Most villagers feel powerless. But we cannot let ourselves be pushed around without doing something to fight back."

Armed with the daring of youth, the rebels, calling themselves the Young Men's Group, sent a petition to the local authorities to have the land deal with the dairy company annulled and set about finding out the dairy farm's next move.

"Information is important. And it's easier for us to find it out than the married men who have families to think about," says Witaya.

According to the villagers, each family is now being offered 5,000 baht to forgive and forget and to turn a blind eye to the next round of land-clearing, an offer topped off with the promise of jobs on the dairy farm.

"They take us for such fools," says farmer Kamjand Techa resentfully. "We have eyes

"The world is changing. You have to be quick-witted to survive."

▼ Harvesting rice

a price on his head of more than 100,000 baht.

"We cannot go about as freely as we want to. We have to go in groups and be more careful of our whereabouts," says Witaya.

Poh Tong, the cattle herder and illiterate father of nine, sighs. "I feel sorry for the kids - and guilty. They are trying to do something, and I can't do anything to help.

"I have to leave home early in the morning with the herd and come back at dusk. It's a bird's life, cattle herding: you only return to your nest to sleep at night. That's why I can't help."

But he feels the cause is in good hands.

"The kids may be young, but they have seen more of the world than us older folks. That makes them wiser.

"The world is changing. Age is no longer important. You have to be quick-witted to survive. On this count, the kids are much better off than us." ■

and ears. They gave the same promises when they took away the common woods in the village next to us. And look what happened there! They fenced in the woods. No one got a job. The villagers now have to bring their cattle to our village common. And they think the same trick will work again."

Patience seems to be running thin on both sides. Rumours are going around that each member of the Young Men's Group has

For Sale: A way of life

▼ Village head
Konkaew Duang-ai

Land *For Sale. 250 square* wah. *Only five million baht.*

The For Sale sign hangs in front of the one-storey brick house of Konkaew Duang-ai, the village head of *Baan* Pong Yang Nok. It is a small village by the Maerim-Samoeng tourist route that meanders through the lush mountains of the Doi Suthep forest reserve in Chiang Mai province.

If the deal goes through, the *poh luang* will become a millionaire overnight.

"I used to be just a poor farmer, struggling hand-to-mouth. I never dreamt of getting out of that rut, let alone touching a million baht. Now, things are getting better by the day," he says, grinning widely with eyes full of hope and enthusiasm.

The nearby road, a pleasantly cool climate and breathtaking scenery have turned the mountain-embraced land along the Maerim route into the prize choice for holiday homes, a raging new status symbol for the rich and famous of Bangkok.

Less than a decade ago, *Baan* Pong Yang Nok farmers would thank their lucky stars if they could get 5,000 baht for one *rai* of land. Now, they are cursing themselves for doing so, because the price for one *rai* exceeds one million baht. But most of the land is already in the hands of speculators.

Fifty-three-year-old *Poh Luang* Konkaew is among the fortunate few who still have some land left.

"If you want to buy, you must move fast," he says, bubbling with the excitement of a stock investor watching a price index rise.

Unfortunately, *Poh Luang* Konkaew's luck is the exception rather that the rule.

Of the 200 families in his village, less than half own some land. Most of those who have sold did so during the early phase of the land boom when the price was much lower. After spending the money they received, many have lapsed into the life of field labourers.

Boon Rattapan is one of them. This 53-year-old farmer sold a plot of six or seven *rai*

of ricefields to a *kamnan* for about 4,000 baht per *rai*. The money was soon used up to pay off debts and buy necessities. *Poh* Boon is now a field labourer, one of the group considered to be on the lowest rung in the village.

The *kamnan* recently sold *Poh* Boon's land for millions of baht.

"The earlier you sell, the worse off you are," comments *Poh Luang* Konkaew, smiling with relief at his own fortune.

"Us peasants didn't know anything then. By the time we did, it was too late. We've helped to make many millionaires."

The landless are hard hit by the land boom. "There is no longer any land for them to rent as tenant farmers. There's not much work left in the fields either, so their families are forced to go off in different directions to find jobs elsewhere," explains the *poh luang*.

The village head brushes aside the myth that the beautiful resorts lining the highway, which are mostly illegal because they have been built in forest reserves, have brought in jobs for the local villagers.

"They prefer to hire hilltribe people," he says, shaking his head wearily, "because they are cheaper and more submissive."

With a recent crackdown on illegal landholding in the forest reserves, land speculators have shied away from the mountain slopes to the valleys to buy up ricefields, using legal tricks and title deeds.

▼ **Hmong hilltribe children**

The *poh luang* lowers his voice to a whisper.

"But they like forest reserves because the land is cheap. One *rai* may cost only 3,000 or 4,000 baht. And then with the power of money, they can get legal documents and extend the area as they please."

Many speculators, he says, started buying land legally from farmers in the valleys, and then extended upwards to include the forest on the surrounding hills, keeping the villagers out in the process.

"They are the *chao nai* , the masters from Bangkok. We cannot say anything," he says, calling the wealthy Bangkokians as most country people do.

He chuckled when asked about forestry officials. "What can they do? If they wanted to arrest someone, they might as well arrest just about everyone, including the villagers. Meanwhile, the masters just keep buying and buying."

Although the villagers know now that patience is golden as the land price continues to rise by the day, many of them are forced to sell their land for fear of it being enclosed.

"Land with no access has no value. So the buying strategy is to gradually buy the outer area first. Then those in the inner area have to sell and they cannot bargain over the price either."

That was why Sri Soodjai sold his five *rai* of land recently. The father of four got two million baht for his plot. His bitterness stems from the knowledge that his land could have fetched many times more than that, yet he could do nothing about it.

According to the deal, he received a first installment of 100,000 baht, the rest to be paid within three months. He knows that by the time the deadline comes, his buyer will have sold the same plot to others for a price he'd rather not know.

All along the resort routes, the air is

▼ *Mae* Kam
  Onpaeng

imbued with the farmers' hopes of a golden chance to leave their life of manual labour and their days in the fields under the merciless sun, to be able to look city people in the eye as equals.

At one resort by another golden tourism route, the Hangdong-Samoeng highway, Kam Onpaeng, a farmer in her 60s, is busy working with flowerpots for garden decoration. But her mind is busy with something else.

The old widow and mother of eight has a three *rai* plot of land near the scenic Maerim route for which the price tag is three million baht.

"My children want me to sell. It's only a small piece of land. Divided among the eight of them, it wouldn't be enough for rice farming or anything else.

"An old man in our village sold his land, because it was too small to divide among his children. He now has a small shop selling knick-knacks. His children have stopped rice farming. They bought pick-up trucks and work as drivers instead."

"I want a better future for my children. I want them to have a good education."

Although *Mae* Kam is pinning her hope of future security on the land deal, the old woman seems regretful at parting with her property.

"But I'm like an old tree by the river. I can fall anytime. I can't work in the ricefields any more and my children no longer want to.

"After giving my children their shares of the land sale, I'll put mine in the bank, so that I will have money to buy rice to eat - I don't eat very much."

Poh Luang Konkaew, however, has seen more than enough to be sceptical of the villagers' eagerness to cash in on the land-selling boom.

"If you don't use the money wisely - and I can tell you that most of them don't - it will disappear in no time at all, and the villagers will slip into more hardship," he says.

Many villagers, he says, give the money to their children to do as they wish: build a new house or buy pick-up trucks and all sorts of electrical appliances. The money is gone before they realise it.

Poh Ging Kannti, aged 53, sold his land six or seven years ago for 200,000 baht, but lost all his share on his pick-up toy. It was confiscated within less than a year, because he could not meet the regular instalment payments.

"It's pick-up truck mania," says *Poh Luang* Konkaew. "The guys all want to make a living from driving, but it doesn't work when everyone thinks the same thing."

But investing the money in farming has proved as disastrous as buying modern status symbols. "With high investment costs and low prices for the crops, which is the situation at the moment, you're soon in debt again."

The best way to use the money, he says, which is what he did, is to buy more land elsewhere, preferably land with good selling prospects.

"It's like exchanging your old small plot of ricefields for a larger one further away," he explains.

Four years ago, he sold three *rai* of ricefields for 500,000 baht. That money got him nine *rai* of land a little further away in Maerim. He sold that to buy 19*rai* up in Chiang Dao.

Poh Luang Konkaew no longer needs to work. He leases his ricefields to tenant farmers in return for half of the produce. With the land boom spreading rapidly in all directions, he knows he can afford to be patient.

He has put up his For Sale sign in front of his house, the last plot in the village, and plans to be five million baht richer.

"No one wants to be farmers all their lives. I want a better future for my children. I want them to have a good education. I want them to be *chao nai* too," he says. "It's only possible when we have money." ∎

Landless after the land boom

Sriwong Wongkham gives a mocking smile when asked if there is any land left in his village to cash in on the land speculation boom.

"We're lucky enough to have land just for our houses," he says. "If anyone is benefiting from the land boom, it's the rich who bought up our farmland a long time ago."

At Buak Koh Hah, Lai Ow and other villages in the vicinity in Lamphun province, most of the land has long been absorbed by the *khon tai,* or the southerners as the northern villagers call Bangkokians and those living downstream.

Although shady, green, longan fruit trees are everywhere in the village of Buak Koh Hah, most of them are owned by a handful of wealthy people from Bangkok and Nakhon Pathom, a province west of Bangkok. Villagers work as gardeners on land that was once theirs.

Of some 160 families in the village, most have only living compounds and make their living as wage earners.

In the dancing heat, it is almost impossible to imagine that Buak Koh Hah was a forest settlement a few decades ago. The big trees went first with the timber concessions. The smaller ones were cut down to feed the ever-hungry charcoal factories and tobacco-curing plants - until there were hardly any trees left.

"That was when we had to start selling our land to survive," recalls 58-year-old Sriwong of the village's gradual loss of land.

Some villagers grew rain-trees in the denuded forest areas to declare ownership of the land as well as to make money from the sealing wax of the lac insects that live on the trees.

But a slump in the price of sealing wax coincided with the longan craze. To ease financial pressures, many villagers sold their land to outsiders looking for orchard land. Others felled their rain-trees to cash in by

"We had to start selling our land to survive."

▼ *Mae* Loy

growing longans themselves.

The villagers' lack of capital, irregular yields and a price slump because of a surplus all added to the gradual selling of orchard land to outsiders.

"Land had no value then," explains Uncle Kong Hankah, who sold his 20 *rai* plot of land five years ago.

"We thought we could make a living by looking after the orchards and doing odd jobs

as well, because the orchards do not need much attention or time."

He got only 30,000 baht for his land, which is now worth millions.

"I needed money to clear my debts, to support my large family and to start anew by raising cattle. I saw no future in rice farming," says the old man as he cuts grass for his cattle in his neighbour's longan orchard.

"I didn't know land would become this

"You've got to be more imaginative when you've got no land to fall back on."

▼ Drying *kah* grass

expensive. If only I had known . . . ," he sighs before continuing his work in silence.

In return for looking after the orchards, villagers usually get ten per cent of the longan yield, normally worth only a few thousand baht. To supplement their income, they work as labourers in the fields. After the rice harvest, the men are hired to cut grass for thatching, while the women bring in extra income by making it into the poor man's roof.

At 50 satang a piece of thatched roof , the women can count on making 20 baht a day.

"You can earn more if you can make your own thatch for sale, not make it for someone else to sell. But it is getting really difficult, because there is no *kah* grass left in the village. You need to have cars and to hire people to go and cut it in far-off villages. But we don't have that kind of money," says *Mae* Loy, an elderly woman, as she threads a blade of thatch grass around a bamboo pole with dextrous fingers.

The more enterprising villagers, however, have turned to trading and acting as middlemen, such as 33-year-old Pranee Moolrangsi.

"There are lots of wild and kitchen vegetables we can sell at the market. And as for thatch, I buy a whole lot of it and make a profit from selling it to market vendors.

"You've got to be more imaginative when you have no land to fall back on," she says.

Despite their landless state, *Baan* Buak Koh Hah villagers consider themselves lucky compared to their neighbours in the adjacent village of Lai Ow. Most of the 32 families there don't even have land for their own houses, but have to share a compound with their relatives and neighbours.

Surrounded by vast fields filled with weeds, the village is hauntingly empty in the daytime. Only the elderly remain to take care of the young, while the able-bodied go out to

▼ **Lai Ow**

work in the fields for 50 baht a day, cutting thatch or working on onion and garlic farms.

"Thatch-making lasts until July," says farmer Nuan Banchai, aged 50. "Then comes the longan harvest season which requires a lot of labour. That will last only until September. After that, we have to look for shrubs and small trees to make firewood for sale until the rice planting season starts, and finally the harvest in December.

"Life is like this, year after year."

Baan Lai Ow was once a forest settlement, like its neighbour. Plagued by ownership insecurity at a time when land still had no legal status and pressed by poverty, the villagers sold their denuded forest land informally on a massive scale to land speculators, one plot after another, until nothing was left.

"We are only peasants. We couldn't say anything when they took more land than they paid us for. We could only watch," says *Poh* Nuan.

▼ Jan Tuesa

any benefit from the land reform project, run on a hire-purchase scheme.

"According to the contract," explains *Poh* Nuan, "I would have had to put in a lot of money to develop the land and pay monthly instalments as well. For city people, the amount of money might not seem much. But for a peasant like me, it would have been impossible. Joining the project would be like enslaving my children to debt. We would never know when we might be freed."

For 54-year-old peasant Jan Tuesa, the hand-to-mouth struggle is a way of life that peasants cannot escape.

"No matter how things change, no matter how valuable the land is, we peasants are always slower than the city people. We're always too late.

The last bout of selling took place as part of a land reform project for landless farmers.

The villagers sold their land to a money baron, who told them that it would be confiscated anyway. They knew they had been cheated when the area was sold to the authorities at a huge profit.

Almost no one in the village received "That's why we have no land left. And that's why we have to continue relying on the only thing we have, our labour.

"It's been like this since the time of our grandfathers and grandmothers. I don't see it getting any better." ∎

Down on the company farm

Farmer Somyot Sutanin likens himself to a baby-corn-growing machine. He explains why.

"A one *rai* plot of land grows 30,000 corn plants. That means 30,000 tassels to strip. And each plant bears three cobs, so that's 90,000 baby corns to pick and more - 90,000 husks to peel off."

All this work is done manually, one cob at a time, adding up to 210,000 separate processes.

The return is 20 baht per kilo of more than 200 cobs - nine satang a cob.

After deducting his outlay on seeds and fertiliser, Somyot earns an average of 14 baht a day, labour and all.

The work takes its toll on the 32-year-old farmer. It's not so much the mind-numbing repetitiveness of the work, but rather the robotic velocity that stretches his human endurance near to breaking point and leaves him in a state of near-collapse at the end of the day.

"We have to work against time, because the baby corns grow so fast, almost by the minute. If we work too slowly, the corns won't be the right size, they'll be too big and they'll be thrown away by the buyers," he says.

"We are like machines, moving through the corn rows, hands above our heads to strip the tassels. Left, right, left, right, until the end of the row. Then turn and back down another row, left, right, left, right.

"It's the same with picking the cobs. We walk between the rows, picking one on the left, then one on the right, again and again. It's burning hot under the sun and itchy walking through the corn blades. My mother used to faint in the middle of working. It was too much for her."

The harvest of the cobs is not the end of their labour. At home, the family will gather round the piles of fresh, green corns to slit the husks with a knife, remove the corn silk and pull out the prized, pearl-white vegetable they have worked so hard for - a finger-sized corn, perfect for canning.

To meet the factory deadline, it is not uncommon for the family to husk the cobs until well after midnight before going out before dawn for another day's work in the fields.

▼ **Traditional form
of transport in
Pah Nod**

To outsiders, this life may seem no better than farm slavery. But to Somyot and other *Baan* Pah Nod villagers, it is the best so far of the various cash crops that have come into their valley in turns.

Once a secluded mountain outpost some 100 kilometres from the northern capital of Chiang Mai, *Baan* Pah Nod is now connected to the outside world by easy roads that roll across mountains, denuded of their natural forest, but separated by ricefields which look like blazing, golden rivers near harvest time.

Although subsistence farming has a long history in this village of 119 families, the farmers' willingness to try any kind of new cash crop introduced by contract farming companies debunks the myth that farmers are resistant to change.

With its cool climate and rich soil,*Baan* Pah Nod, like many other northern villages,

"I couldn't put up with the uncertainty of crop prices any longer."

has been visited by representatives of various contract farming companies, each making new offers of crop varieties to feed the growing agro-industry.

The average land ownership in the village is less than one *rai*, which makes it impossible for farmers to depend on rice alone and forces them to make full use of the land after the rice harvest.

Experiments with ginger, chillies, peanuts, tomatoes, string beans and many other cash crops have fizzled out, one after the other.

Contract farming, Thai-style, is based on verbal promises. The villagers' repeated disappointments are epitomised by the string bean tragedy, as farmer Pat Apaimool explains, his voice ringing with resentment.

"The company provided the seeds in advance and promised to buy the beans at an agreed price.

"They kept their word, but not for long. They started selling us fertilisers and pesticides which they said we had to use to produce a standard quality of produce. And then for no reason, they just disappeared. We could not sell the beans, because everybody was growing the same thing. We just had to let the plants die in the fields," says the 35-year-old farmer.

Then about six years ago came baby corn, the cash crop that has lasted the longest.

"It's easier to grow and take care of than other crops," says Somyot. "It doesn't need chemical pesticides, so it's safe and more economical. And it's fast. Only 45 days after planting, we can sell the corn and get money or use them ourselves for cattle feed."

The villagers feel that baby corn offers a viable and attractive alternative to tobacco farming which, although more profitable, invites slow death because of the extensive use of chemical pesticides.

Pat gave up tobacco farming because the 12 years of chemical pesticide use had started to take its toll on his health.

"I was constantly tired and dizzy. My limbs were getting weak. I lost my appetite. Some of my neighbours with similar symptoms died, and the doctors said it was because of the pesticides. So I quit, simply because I'm afraid of death," says the father of two.

Unlike most *Baan* Pah Nod farmers, who are cashing in on baby corn, Pat decided to turn his back on cash crops and try his luck with integrated farming.

"I couldn't put up with the uncertainty of crop prices any longer," he complains. "Not once have we got the prices that I thought we would get. And no matter what we do to try to reduce our outlay, the buyers always have the upper hand."

To meet factory standards, the farmers are told to use the company's seeds, crop

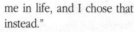

▼ **Gathering crops**

hormones, fertilisers and pesticides.

"We tried to develop our own seeds, but they didn't work. I don't know what they do to their seeds, but the quality of the crops drops after the first yield.

"As for chemical pesticides, we tried to develop a cheaper mixture of our own for tobacco. But the company just wouldn't buy our tobacco leaves, because they said they were below standard. So we had to buy pesticides from them again. They control everything."

It was not until his wife fell sick that Pat decided to quit cash crop farming, contract style, once and for all.

"I was worried about my wife, but the baby corn had to come first. The cobs have to be picked at the same hour of the day, come rain or shine, and husked the same day. One day absent and you lose the whole batch.

"I felt so depressed. What is the use of working so hard? What is the point of working like a machine when it does not allow you the time even to care for people important to you? " Suddenly, I realised what mattered to

me in life, and I chose that instead."

At Pat's spacious wooden house, attesting to the richness that was once in the forests of *Baan* Pah Nod, the cool water for his guests comes from earthen water jars, not a refrigerator. He travels to other villages on his old bicycle, not by pick-up truck. A plate of *miang*, traditional preserved tea leaves, to be chewed with salt, is offered as a gesture of hospitality.

"I'm contented," he says. "But I think these days, we country folk are plagued with feelings of inferiority. We try to be like the city people too much. That's why we are entangled in so many problems."

His kitchen garden provides his family not only with daily food, but also with unexpected petty cash because the other farmers, who grow corn, have no time to spare to grow their own food, so must buy it all. Pat has also begun growing a variety of trees bearing fruit and edible leaves. He keeps cattle and is planning to dig fishponds to provide his family with a secure source of food.

"I'm no longer a slave of deadline pressures. I can work at my own pace. I can rest

"Life is possible without relying on cash crops."

and do things with my family. I have time for my neighbours and for the community. Our health is better than ever. I can save 42 baht every month for the family. Life is possible without relying on cash crops."

Although Pat's way of farming represents new hope, he remains an exception.

"I could not do that," says another farmer, 37-year-old Prasert Jampop, quickly brushing aside the idea of giving up cash crops. "I have my debts to think about. I've got to think of how best to get money to free myself from them first."

Although the deadline pressures of baby corn cultivation do not allow the villagers to help one another out in farming as they used to, it is different when it comes to group interests.

In the village baby corn network that *Baan* Pah Nod is part of, the *kamnan*, the subdistrict head, is the sub-contractor for the company. He chooses men in the different villages, often the village headmen, to be the buyers of the corn for those villages.

"We want to have direct contact with the factories," says farmer Wirat Singbee. "But that is impossible, because we don't know where they are, and even if we did, they wouldn't want to deal directly with us."

They say the *kamnan* gets 25 baht for a kilogramme of baby corn from the company, but he gives only 20 baht to the villagers.

Acting as a group, however, the villagers succeeded in pressuring their village buyer to give them 50 satang per kilo more. The extra money is being used to set up a central village fund for emergency use.

But their bargaining has not been without problems. The village buyer gave the same higher price to farmers outside the group as well to undermine its collective strength.

As the bargaining goes on, farmers continue to look around for other cash crops. Baby corn prices have been the same for years, but the cost of fertiliser is rising steadily.

"For now, baby corn is still good. But we don't know how long it'll last," says farmer Prasert. "We have to keep our eyes and ears open."

Along the hilly, orange road, one can see plots of other corn-like plants, which are used for broom-making, and the Japanese *suiyo* melon, grown for export.

But the villagers say they have learned to be more cautious. Conversations with people from other villages have taught them that *suiyo* melon is good only for a few years before the soil is spoiled.

"But we must keep on trying new things," says Prasert. "We have the labour, the time, the land. The companies have the money. If we don't try, we'll never know what will work and what won't. We're in too deep. We can't ⟩ stop now." ■

Warning: Tobacco growing damages your health

▼ **Aunt Sook Sakham sorts tobacco leaves**

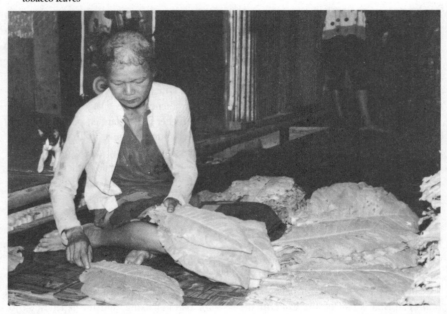

Aunt Sook Sakham used to be a vivacious, outgoing matron. She rarely missed the meetings of the village women's group. In activities of the local temple, Aunt Sook was always the woman in charge.

Now she has buried herself away at home.

" I don't want people to see me like this," she says, slowly running her fingers through her scalp which looks like the bald head of a worn-out, plastic doll with only a few scant strands of hair on it.

"My hair used to be long and thick. I took it for granted. And now this, " she sighs. "This has destroyed

▼ **Boon Jaiban**
grows beans
▼ **Boon Jaiban**

my life."

The 45-year-old tobacco farmer is not the only victim of the prolonged abuse of chemical pesticides in the farm community of *Baan* Saluangnai in Chiang Mai province, which, like most villages in the North, relies on tobacco as its main cash crop.

People think smoking is bad for your health. For the

tobacco farmers, the dangers are far worse.

Uncle Boon Wongdee, aged 58, has also become bald after years and years of spraying chemical pesticides in his tobacco fields, a routine that leaves the farmer completely soaked with the hazardous liquid.

Fifty-year-old Uncle Tah Pohkham, who lives in

nearby *Baan* Kad Hao village, fainted during his spraying routine and was almost paralysed.

Even the village head of *Baan* Saluangnai has not escaped the health calamity wrought by the chemicals. Once an avid advocate of "new agriculture", as villagers call chemical intensive farming, he gave up tobacco farming after developing chronic dizziness and respiratory complications, common symptoms among the tobacco farmers.

The list of victims is endless. After some 30 years of tobacco farming, the villagers no longer question the dangers of chemical pesticides. The question now is, What is a viable alternative to tobacco when they are hard pressed by debts and cash pressures?

Baan Saluangnai, a farm community of 165 families, is only a short drive from the town of Chiang Mai. But a car has to travel at a snail's pace, rocking to and fro like an ox-pulled cart as it climbs the rugged, dusty road through the hills to the village.

The brisk, clear air, however, makes all the colours of the surroundings stand out in bright cheerfulness. The sky is the bluest of blues. The ripe ricefields that await harvesting are ablaze with gold. The harvested ones are yellow-brown with rice stems. Newly-ploughed plots of land, ready for cash crops, are of such a rich, deep brown that one can almost smell their fresh fragrance.

Boon Jaibaan, well-covered from head to toe to protect himself from the sun, complete with sunglasses and gloves, is resting for lunch during the harvest chores. A big, portable stereo on an earthen dyke fills the fields with the music of Bangkok's latest pop hits. Men and women laughingly cajole one another as they help themselves to preserved tamarind from a plastic bag to ease a thirst that has come from working long hours in the sun.

Boon, a father of two, says he quit growing tobacco after the rice harvest five years ago.

"I'm afraid for my life," says the 39-year-

"Spraying is like taking a bath in chemical pesticide."

old farmer. Nearly 30 years of using chemical pesticide has taken its toll on the community and himself.

Tobacco was one of the first, popular cash crops that came to the North in the contract farming system. A national Tobacco Monopoly law requires farmers to sell their produce only to companies which have been granted concessions by the government. This means that the farmers have to comply with every rule and regulation set up by the concessioners' curing plants to ensure crop standardisation.

"At first, we used natural fertilisers and our own indigenous varieties of pesticides," explains another farmer, Somkid Yasaeng, aged 33. "Then all the curing plants started to tell us to use this and that which we could only get from them, at their fixed prices. They give us the chemicals in advance and deduct the cost later when we sell the tobacco to them. And they send their people round regularly to check that we're using their stuff. If not, they refuse to buy our tobacco, saying that it is substandard."

Before growing the tobacco saplings, the farmers are required to use a chemical to kill off any grass and to put a special, fungi-killing chemical in each hole dug for the plants. After that, they have to spray the vulnerable plants regularly to protect them from pests.

Somkid also quit growing tobacco because of the health risks involved.

"When the plants get big and their leaves become intertwined over our heads, we have to walk through the dense rows slowly to spray each one of them thoroughly. When there's a breeze, the spray blows back over us, but we have to keep on going. Before we're done, we're soaking wet. It's like taking a bath in chemical pesticide," he explains.

The harvest is no less dangerous.

Ideally, for a harvest to be safe, the leaves should be cut at least two weeks after a chemical spraying.

"But if we were to wait that long, we wouldn't be able to make a living. As soon as the company places its order, we have to make our tobacco leaves ready, even if we only sprayed them the previous day," says Boon.

The leaves are cut early in the morning, usually by the women. As they carefully bury their heads in the dense rows, looking for the right leaves, the dew mixed with poisonous chemicals seeps into their scarves where it stays in contact with their scalps for hours, day in, day out.

When Aunt Sook's head first began to feel itchy, she thought she had lice. When the itching became so intolerable, she decided to wash her hair with detergent. When it still persisted, she thought a chemical perm would

▼ *Mae* **Khangaew**
Tongmoon

help.

"But then, I felt as if my head were being burnt with hot water. After that, my hair began to come off in big handfulls, until it got to be the way it is now," she says sighing.

Besides dangers to themselves, the farmers don't have any doubts either about the deadly impact of the chemicals on their natural environment.

"Birds die because they eat dead toads. The toads die because they dig their holes and eat the fungi-killing chemicals. When cats or dogs eat those birds, they also die. Its touch is deadly," says Somkid.

The first fatal sign, however, came from the fish in the

"I know growing tobacco is dangerous. But I can't afford to change."

ricefields and in the creeks.

"We've noticed that the fish look wounded, every kind of fish -*pla chon, pla salid, pla tapian, pla dook,* even *pla lai.* They look like lepers. And things have got much more serious over the past five years," says Somkid.

With these fatal effects now so apparent, many villagers at *Baan* Saluangnai have opted to grow beans instead of tobacco, although their earnings per *rai* are about 2,000 baht less.

"We've got to face it. No farmer can avoid using chemicals to up the yields. But we just have to choose a crop with lower risks," says Boon.

The bean's height, only knee high, makes it safer for farmers to use chemical spray. As to frequency, beans need no more than four sprayings in one season, while tobacco has to be sprayed every seven days. While some farmers are now successfully using herbal pesticides on their beans, such efforts to increase health safety and reduce costs are off-limits to tobacco farmers because of the contract farming rules.

Although less profitable, the market and price security of beans at the moment has helped the farmers to make a change of crop at a time when death is staring them in the face.

Not everyone, however, can afford to quit growing tobacco, even though it means slow death.

The reason is short and simple - money.

Uncle Tah went right back to growing tobacco after recovering from his severe illness, knowing full well he could collapse again and perhaps become paralysed.

"I simply cannot change to other crops. Tobacco is the fastest. You can get money within 60 days. And the money is better than with beans," he explains, but his cringed brows and fretting eyes show his nagging worries.

"I simply have to be more careful not to spray the pesticides in the sun or work too long. And if I feel dizzy, I drink sugar cane juice to ease it. That's all I can do."

Although it's nearly dusk, *Mae* Khangaew Tongmoon, aged 41, is still busy raking the soil, preparing the land for another cash crop after the rice harvest.

It's for tobacco.

"I know it's dangerous. But what can I do? I have the children's schooling to think about," she explains, sweat glistening on her forehead.

Then she sighs and gives a long pause before continuing.

"I really don't know. I might have to change one of these days. I'm worried too for my health and for my children. Probably I'll do it next year. Probably. But not now. I can't afford it now." ■

Cabbage worse than opium poppies

▼ *Pob* Mah
Muenjai

C abbage is worse than poppies - or so the angry farmers of Chomthong district in Chiang Mai province think. "It's much worse," says farmer Mah Muenjai, aged 55, a community dam leader who is in charge of water management in ten villages in the district, covering over 10,000 *rai* of land.

"For poppies, the hilltribes need only a small piece of land. They can grow the flowers only once a year and don't need to use any pesticides.

"When they grow poppies, we lowlanders have abundant water for our farmland. The streams are safe to drink and use. We can just live and let live, as we've always done.

"For cabbages, however, the hilltribe people need to clear a lot of the forest for the land to make it profitable. They use rotating sprinklers to shower the cabbage plots all day long with chemical pesticides. And they grow cabbages all year round.

"So now, the river is running dry because of massive deforestation. We are bankrupt because we cannot farm any more. The fish are dying because of the polluted water. Our buffaloes get sores if they swim in the creeks.

We get diarrhoea and dizziness if we drink the water.

"In my lifetime, I've never experienced so much hardship. That's why I say, compared to poppies, the hilltribes' cabbage is worse."

The cabbage war between the lowland rice farmers of Chomthong district, covering thousands of *rai* of farmland, and the cabbage-growing hilltribes, largely Hmong people, has been raging for several years without a solution.

Resentment is widespread of what the lowlanders feel is the government's tacit support of the hilltribes in the name of anti-narcotics programmes through cash crop substitution, without paying attention to consequent adverse environmental repercussions.

"And if they think that the hilltribes are abandoning opium cultivation for cabbage, then they're fooling themselves," says one villager sarcastically. "You don't have to walk deep in the forest to find that out."

Their anger is escalating as villagers threaten to take matters into their own hands if the state continues to allow the hilltribes to cultivate in the rain catchment mountains.

Doi Inthanon, the highest mountain

▼ **Carpets of cabbage grow on the mountain slopes**

range in Thailand and a national park, is the source of many waterways which feed thousands of *rai* of farmland in Chomthong and nearby districts.

A drive up the mountain brings out mixed feelings.

The lush greenery at the foot of the mountain is delightful as the road spirals upward in the fresh, fragrant air of the forests. The bright yellow of wild sunflowers is sprinkled along the roadsides, which overlook a vast golden valley below where Karens, another hilltribe people, are working in their ricefields under clear blue skies.

Pick-up trucks, full of cabbages, pass in the opposite direction, heading down to the district market.

As the road continues upward, the dense tropical jungle gradually

"People must not be allowed to farm in the watershed area."

▼ A pick-up truck
loads up with
cabbages

turns into a pine forest. Then, all of a sudden, there are denuded mountains all around.

Unlike the Karens, whose rotating system of farming limits the number of trees they cut down, the Hmongs' slash-and-burn cultivation has made them the main culprits of deforestation in the eyes of lowland farmers.

The Hmongs' more entrepreneurial spirit, which has made them quicker than other tribes to adopt cash crops, introduced by Thai and foreign agencies as opium crop substitutes, has also made them the Chomthong farmers' direct enemies.

At *Baan* Khun Klang, one of the Hmong villages on Doi Inthanon mountain, the valleys and hill slopes are covered with green carpets of cabbages. It is the watershed area of the Mae Klang river, but everywhere one turns, it's cabbage - on the hills, in the valleys, piled up at the roadside, ready to be loaded onto pick-up trucks, which come down from the deeper hills where cabbages are planted on an even more massive scale.

To give the vegetable its luxuriously fresh and green look, blue plastic pipes pierce

and snake through the orange mountain terrain before rearing their heads above ground over the cabbage plots to sprinkle the venomous liquid onto the crop all day long to keep pests away.

The heavy use of chemical pesticides has taken a serious toll on the Hmong farmers' health.

"Many elderly farmers have developed serious skin problems," says a village teacher. "Some also have swollen feet and hands. The young farmers still have resistance to the chemicals, but not the elderly."

The hilltribe growers, fully aware of the health hazards, do not eat the chemically-bathed cabbages themselves, but send them directly to the vegetable market in Bangkok for city consumers.

The obvious environmental effects of deforestation have prompted Chomthong village leaders to form a watershed conservation group, headed by the dam masters in the area.

"Our work used to be to mobilise villagers to repair the dams, damaged by the strong, overflowing currents.

"Now, the rivers have all become dry

"We have to end the deforestation before it ends us."

and shallow. We've got to get together to dig the river bed. Things are turning upside down," says dam master *Poh* Mah.

A few years ago, the angry conservation group put up a wire fence around a watershed forest in Mae Soy district to stop the hilltribes from felling trees.

The confrontation almost ended in violence.

"Since the officials are paying no heed, we have to take matters into our own hands," says *Poh* Suwit Namtep, head of the Chomthong watershed conservation group.

Water scarcity has made chemical contamination of the river all the more serious, rendering the water no longer drinkable.

But it is the lack of farm water that hits the lowlanders most.

Massive land clearing and water retention up in the mountains for the vast cabbage fields has led to serious water shortages in the lowlands. Year-round cultivation, characteristic of the North because of limited land, is now impossible.

Many farmers have wound up bankrupt. Others have sold their land to speculators to clear their debts.

"Very soon, land speculators will take over our whole area, all because we can no longer make a living as farmers," says *Poh* Suwit.

The watershed conservation group has sent petitions to the authorities several times, asking them to relocate the hilltribes from the watershed areas, but to no avail.

Despite promises, the controversy is at a deadlock, due to the political complexities involved. Not only is unused, good land hard to find, but relocation would mean a painful change in the traditional way of life of the hilltribes.

But the Chomthong villagers remain adamant.

Their complaints about the contamination and shortage of water, which used to be brushed aside as hearsay, have been lent weight by an increasing number of academic research studies.

"The authorities have got to be more farsighted," says *Poh* Suwit. "They cannot just try to solve one problem, the hilltribes growing opium poppies, and create many others in the process, without paying attention."

The Chomthong farmers' group say they will fight to the end to defeat the cabbage monster.

"Our basic demand remains the same: people must not be allowed to farm in the watershed area.

"The forest is most important for our survival. The forest is our second parent," he says.

"We have to end the deforestation before it ends us." ■

"Go South" young girl

T here are hardly any young girls left in the small rice farming village of *Baan* Srijomjaeng in Phayao province.

After completing compulsory schooling up to Grade 6 at the age of 12 or so, the girls go to work in Bangkok or the southern towns of Had Yai, Sungai Kolok or Betong - all

centres of the flesh trade. Almost always, they go with the consent of their parents, who receive advance payment for their daughters' work.

The tragedy lies in the fact that *Baan* Srijomjaeng is no exception. It is just a typical village among thousands in the North.

Why do parents sell their daughters?

Why do they let their girls, as young as 13, be sexually violated at the whim of strangers?

Is it hunger? Poverty? Or is it greed?

All such questions have to be

◄ An old wooden
house in
Srijomjaeng
▼ Guan Somyong
and family in
front of their
concrete house

"My daughter saw the family suffer and she wanted to help."

▼ **Pon Chaitep**

swallowed when coming face-to-face with Pon Chaitep, a peasant who let his daughter go to work as a prostitute in Sungai Kolok, a town on the Malaysian border, in exchange for 15,000 baht.

The old man's face is dry, shrivelled and lifeless. He talks quietly, his eyes almost always pinned to the ground. He walks as if he is afraid to hurt the soil. His back bends, probably from never having had a chance to walk upright as other people's equal.

At village meetings, his place is in the back row. At a drink around the bonfire at night, his place is outside the circle, far from the fire. His glass is filled only at the generosity of others. And he sits as he always does, turned in upon himself, arms folded close to his chest, coughing asthmatically, his body shrunken as if he wished he might disappear into thin air.

"I didn't sell my daughter," mumbles the father of eight apologetically. "She saw me suffer. She saw the family suffer. And she wanted to help."

In the world of the subsistence farmer, everyone must contribute to the family's survival. Saving face and dignity come from fulfilling your duty to extract your family from this daily struggle.

A village of some 80 families, *Baan* Srijomjaeng depends solely on rain-fed rice farming. The weeds, turning red because of the dust, play in the wind on the vast fields that lie idle for seven months of the year until the rains come around again.

Prostitution is the only immediately accessible means for an uneducated country girl to help free her family from hardship when rice farming is not enough to live on. She has no ready alternative either but to sell her body if she is to secure for them some of the benefits of modern life that city people take so much for granted and which rural

"I couldn't stop her. I have nothing better to give her."

people want to have too.

It is now considered virtuous in some villages for a woman to sacrifice herself for her family.

So Uncle Pon's daughter left. But the decision was not made overnight.

Day in, day out, Pon and his family walk past their neighbours' brightly-coloured, concrete houses, the kind they have seen on television or in well-thumbed magazines which have passed through countless hands before coming to the village.

The houses, paid for by the girls' remittances, are evidence of a daughter's virtue: her readiness to sacrifice herself, her gratitude to her parents and, more importantly, her success.

Standing in stark contrast to the villagers' old, wooden houses and thatched huts, these concrete houses have become monuments of temptation that constantly remind other peasants of what might have been - or what might be.

When they travel outside the village, they see more and more of these big, concrete houses, sprouting up along the main Phayao highway - no need to ask where the money came from.

They watch the successful girls visiting home with a new life-style and a new-found confidence, of the kind they so admire in city people.

Meanwhile, the procurers, mostly old hands with city connections who have returned to the village, keep coming by with their offers.

"It was when we were about to lose our ricefields because of the drought that my daughter decided to go," says Uncle Pon quietly, showing no anger at a stranger's intrusion on his private wounds.

"I couldn't stop her. I have nothing better to give her."

The deal is understood between the girls, their parents and the brothel owners. The girls are bonded to the brothel. They must pay back double the amount that their parents are paid in advance when their daughters first leave the village. The girls themselves receive nothing until they have done so.

It was not until a year after she had left that Uncle Pon received money directly from his daughter.

"I couldn't use it for anything substantial. It all went on food and medicine. I'm not well, and there are the hungry mouths of the little ones to feed."

If Uncle Pon is submissive, it's because, more than anything, he feels he is the picture of failure.

His daughter stopped working to marry a waiter in the hotel where she worked. She also stopped sending money. In the lottery of life, Uncle Pon's daughter missed the prize.

▼ Guan Somyong
and family

Not so the daughters of Guan Somyong. His wide, happy grin tells all.

The beginning of Uncle Guan's story is the same as Uncle Pon's, only the ending is different.

"Our family suffered so much before this," says Guan, relaxing in the warm, morning sun in front of his one-storey, concrete house.

Like Uncle Pon, Guan is at first taken aback by the insolence of a stranger who dares to ask about what the villagers consider a private matter.

But the stranger is from Bangkok, a guest to be welcomed, someone of the city culture he looks up to, someone who dresses and talks in the manner his daughter aspires to. So he lets his story flow with the confidence that comes with money, the kind that Uncle Pon would dearly love to have.

"My daughter, Riam, left when she was 15, the first girl in the village to go.

"The agent contacted her three times. I didn't let her go at first. I even went so far as to get her a motorcycle to convince her to stay.

"But she insisted that she couldn't bear to see the family go hungry. She said she would support the family herself.

"She said if I didn't let her go, she would escape anyway. If she had done that, I wouldn't have known where she was. So I decided to go with her, to see for myself where and how she would live, to make sure she was safe."

Riam's mother recalled the scene when her daughter left.

"All the relatives came to stop her, but she wouldn't listen. We were all in tears. I'll never forget that."

Being the first girl to leave meant that Riam's family had to bear the heaviest humiliation.

"I felt so ashamed," recalls her mother. "I stopped seeing people for months. I couldn't eat. I couldn't sleep. I was afraid for my child's safety. I was afraid of the neighbours' scorn. I was a wreck."

Money stopped all the gossip. The message was clear. The risk that Riam had taken had paid off.

"Now all the girls want to go," she says with laughter that has a triumphant ring to it.

Riam has given her father more than a house, a television set, a refrigerator and a stereo. She has made him someone in the community.

He was once a landless peasant, one of those who sat in the back row at village meetings. Now he sits at the front. At social gatherings, he is the one who pays for the drinks.

"Having money is definitely good," says Uncle Guan with certainty. "It means we don't have to go about asking people for loans. We don't have to go through all that humiliation."

He laughs heartily when asked about his status in the village now. "I don't know. You've got to ask others, not me," he says. The old man was recently appointed supervisor of the temple's funds, a position given only to the village's most trustworthy person.

He and his wife talk about Riam with obvious pride.

"She is a good daughter. She takes care of us in our old age."

Colour photographs of her adorn the living room wall, in various happy poses like a movie star, wearing make-up and brightly-coloured clothes. She is a beauty, the picture of happiness.

There is no longer hunger and poverty in the family. So why did they send her younger sister away?

"We didn't," Guan replies with a firm shake of his head. "She wanted to work. There was nothing for her to do at home. She saw how Riam was able to send home money. We were afraid she would run away, so we sent her to stay with her sister in Bangkok.

"We did not force our daughters to go. We never did."

But now, because of the AIDS scare, Uncle Guan has called his two daughters back to the village. Riam's Japanese boyfriend gives her 10,000 baht a month, which she dutifully hands over to her parents.

Her younger sister has just married a salesman and gives her parents 5,000 baht a month.

"I never waste my daughters' money, unlike other parents. That's why they end up having nothing. I save the money to build houses and buy ricefields. It's not for myself. It's for my children's future. Everything will go to my children when I'm gone," says Uncle Guan.

"Money is definitely good," he reaffirms. His wife nods. In the deadening silence that follows, no one dares contradict him. ∎

"I didn't sell my daughter"

Fifteen-year-old In Wonglah left her village home on the hill two months ago. Her mother, Moon, received 2,000 baht in return.

Moon looks like a frightened deer when asked about her daughter.

"No, I didn't sell my child. I didn't." Her voice trembles. She looks at her mother-in-law sitting nearby, appealing for support.

In the flicker of candlelight within her bamboo hut, its thin walls pierced by the cold air, the pale-looking woman begins to sob quietly. Her two small children sleep on the floor, bundled up for warmth in a ragged blanket.

"I didn't sell her. I just borrowed money. She is working to pay off the debt. She'll come home soon," she says, her voice breaking between sobs.

Mae Da, her mother-in-law, looks lost. But with Moon unable to control herself, the old woman explains the situation. Her eyes show uncertainty, a mixture of fear and hope. It does not take long to find out why.

"My son, Moon's husband, was arrested a year ago for cutting trees. He has to stay in jail for seven years, even though he's not guilty. He's just a scapegoat. But now we have no one to take care of us.

"My daughter-in-law, Moon, is all by herself. I'm too old to help in the fields, so my granddaughter left to work as a maid. There is nothing wrong with that.

"We suffer so much. Probably you can help. Can you get my son out of prison, please?"

Baan Huay Chompoo, an ethnic Lua community up on a hill in Chiang Rai province, is no stranger to fear, insecurity and inferiority. Its villagers stand on the bottom rung of ethnic prejudice. They defer to the northerners, who in turn defer to government officials and city people. For the Lua peasants, all these people are their *chao nai,* their

"I didn't sell her. I just borrowed money. She is working to pay off the debt."

▼ **A bamboo hut in Huay Chompoo**

masters to be feared.

Their fear and insecurity is heightened by their illegal jobs.

The low yields they derive from rice farming on the hills only last them the few months after the harvest. But there is dense forest nearby, so they earn money by cutting down trees, sometimes on their own initiative, but more often in the pay of influential people with connections.

Forestry officials often raid their villages for illegally cut wood, which villagers argue they keep to build their houses or sell in times of emergency. The last raid netted several villagers, including *Mae* Da's two sons and one son-in-law.

"It's unfair. Why don't they arrest the people who hired my children? I hate them," laments *Mae* Da.

While the men are out risking their freedom by illegally cutting trees, the young girls "go South," a euphemism for working as prostitutes, to prise the family out of the trap of hardship and contempt because of their poverty.

Theirs is the often repeated story of

▼ A new house in
Huay Chompoo

prostitution in the North of Thailand. It takes a girl or two to break the rigid cultural taboo. When everyone sees the immediate improvement in living standards that the girls bring to their families, all hell breaks loose, and everyone wants to go.

The first girl left *Baan* Huay Chompoo about ten years ago, just about the same time as modern development reached the village.

To push the hill people into the modern age and to make them give up their old, so-called uncivilised ways, officials set up an agricultural centre - now forsaken - a school and a Buddhist temple. Battery-powered televisions beamed the glossy life of Bangkok right into their huts.

"Since the school was set up, we have no longer worn our traditional clothes," recalls Wan Tankhiaw, a mother of four and another daughter-in-law of *Mae* Da. "We hill people are shy. In the market, for example, other people used to look at us as if we were freaks. We want to dress like them."

There are now only two pieces of traditional, hand-woven Lua cloth left in the village, dating back over three generations. None

▼ A young girl of
Huay Chompoo

of the young girls today knows how to weave. They opt for mass-produced clothes, as they opt for plastic ornaments over their traditional silver ones.

A legend of their tribe, the most numerous and warlike in the days before the kingdoms of Chiang Rai and Chiang Mai, does not help the remaining Lua feel especially good about themselves.

"Lua comes from *la* in our Lisu language which means 'being left behind'," says *Mae* Da. "God told the northerners and us to go to see him, so that he could give us all land. On the way, we stopped to boil clams and wait for them to soften up, so we were late. God gave all the good land to the *khon muang*, the northern city people. We were so stupid."

In the past, she says, the Lua people were usually conscripted as soldiers when fighting broke out between the northern kingdoms.

"That's why most of us have been killed off. Our elders used to say that we Lua do not have to work so much for the country, because we have done too much in the past."

Mae Da's spirits rise as she drifts away from present misery, back into past glory. But the moment does not last long.

Her worries are for her sons, not her granddaughter.

"My granddaughter is fine. She wrote us a letter saying so and telling us we had no need to worry about her. She said she had enough food and was living well. It's good. She does not have to labour in the sun like us.

"But my sons. How they are going to live for seven years in prison?"

Moon has now recovered herself, although there are dry tearstains on her face.

"I'm just a woman," she says. "I have four children to feed. How can I do that without a man in the family ?

"My husband and I had never been parted. My heart broke after he went to jail. I have been living in constant fear since then. I never used to be like that. I'm so afraid of what

▼ Huay Chompoo village

the future might bring."

She sent her first son to stay at the village temple to save the family from having another mouth to feed. That was after he and his sister refused to go to school one day because they did not have the sports uniform required by the school. The boy's clothes cost 70 baht and the girl's 55 baht, but Moon's daily wage, which goes mostly on food, is only 40 baht.

Moon shakes her head vigorously, refusing any suggestion that her daughter might soon be forced to work as a prostitute. Her boss is a brothel owner, the husband of one of the first batch of *Baan* Huay Chompoo girls to go South.

"That's impossible. My daughter is still very tiny. They told me they only needed her to help wash the dishes and clean the house," insists Moon.

The brothel owner's mother-in-law lives in the village. It was she who proposed that Moon should send her daughter South with two other girls. In return, the procurer receives 2,000 baht commission a head, a lucra-tive business in this vicin-ity.

Moon, nervous as ever, refuses to name her. The woman is also a money lender. To anger her in any way means to lose access to a source of ready cash that might be needed in the future.

Wan reveals her sis-ter-in-law's secrets in a whisper. "They promised her that if she let her daughter go, they would help get her husband out of jail. She needed any help she could get."

Moon fiercely hangs on to the belief that her daughter is safe. "She wrote to us that she was fine," she says. "I didn't want to let her go. But she wanted to. She wanted to help.

"That's why I only asked her boss for 2,000 baht. That's all I needed to buy rice and food. They offered 10,000 baht for her. But I didn't want her to have to work too long to pay off the debt. I want her to come back home.

"I miss my child. I miss my husband. You don't know how I suffer. I feel helpless trying to make ends meet, struggling on my own. You don't know what it's like." ■

Akha village breaking down

Within a few years, the mountaintop Akha village of Mae Poen in Chiang Rai province will be no more.

Ten years ago, it was a popular stop on the Chiang Rai tourist trekking routes. It was blessed with an exotic culture and forest greenery. Although accessible only on foot, it is not too far from the highway.

Today, the forest is gone. The villagers' Akha culture and traditions are all but forgotten. The tourists stopped coming long ago. Even the village itself may vanish; the easy access to the main road, at first seen as a blessing, has brought an avalanche of change that threatens to sweep it away.

"I don't think we can stay here much longer. Land is most important to our livelihood, and there's almost none of it left," says Atoloh, son of the village leader.

Of the 1,000 *rai* of farm land allocated by the authorities to the hilltribes at *Baan* Mae Poen, some 800 *rai* have been gobbled up by land speculators, cashing in on the land boom in Chiang Rai.

The remaining land is the hilltop site of the village. But money barons, working

▼ **Atoloh and
his son**

through local officials, are pressuring the Akhas to sell even this and just go away.

It's an offer they cannot refuse. Their options are to take the money and go or end up being moved elsewhere by the authorities anyway, without compensation.

"I'm angry. But what can I do? I'm too afraid of them," grumbles Akoh, an Akha elder, bitterly, who lost his farm land to speculators.

"If I hadn't sold, they would have used their influence to chase me away anyway. They can do anything they want to us.

"Being hill people, we have so many disadvantages. People from the lowlands use their laws, which we don't know about, to get at us.

"The townspeople are so cruel. They threaten us all the time and we cannot fight back.

"It's not good for hill people and lowlanders to have close contact with one another. Why can't we just live and let live, like we used to?"

A deep sigh says, however, that Akoh knows full well why not.

Like other hilltribes, the Akhas at *Baan* Mae Poen live in a state of insecurity, because they are constantly fearful of being resettled by the authorities. They live in a state of inferiority to lowlanders and of frustration at being blamed for the problems in the North of

▼ Akoh, an
Akha elder

deforestation and narcotic drugs.

Their lack of legal status as non-Thais in Thailand and the fact that they are so ill-informed makes them easy prey to threats and abuse. It aggravates animosity and exacerbates their feelings of helplessness and of being for ever at the mercy of outsiders' whims.

Of the 300 or so hilltribe people in the village of Mae Poen, fewer than 30 have received Thai citizenship. The rest cannot travel outside the district without official approval. If they do, it's at their own risk.

Opium-smoking, still an open secret in most hilltribe villages, also makes them vulnerable targets.

"The police can come up here any time to search our houses or arrest us. How can you expect the elderly villagers to give up smoking just like that? We often have to pay the police to avoid problems. They just want our money," says one villager.

The rolling, rugged road leading to *Baan* Mae Poen slowly makes its way across the vast terrain of starkly, denuded hills. There are simply no signs of what only 20 years ago was a cool, dense forest. Along the way, there are lychee and longan orchards on either side instead. The knee high saplings show that the invasion is new. Fences have been put up on what was once the hilltribes' common land to define the territories of new owners. Each orchard has a name, beautifully inscribed on

▼ **Akha woman
of Mae Poen**

a sign. After passing a rose farm and tourist resort, the road comes to the back of the hilltop village.

"The main road to the front entrance of our village is closed now," explains Atoloh. "A group of land speculators bought up all the land on both sides at the mouth of the road. Then they closed it down to fence it in, so they could force people living further along to sell their land."

The land problems started three years ago with the beginning of the land boom in Chiang Rai, following the building of the multi-million-baht Chiang Rai airport and plans to make the province another tourist centre.

"It was the northerners with their power and influence who forced us to sell. They said that if we didn't, they could move us any time they wanted," says Atoloh. "It's because of this fear that we let go of our land. We had no choice."

The conflicts with land speculators are obviously far from over.

While Atoloh is talking, a group of young men zoom up on motorcycles to watch from a distance. They are the *kamnan's* men.

"You'd better not stay here overnight," whispers Atoloh. "I cannot guarantee anyone's safety. The *kamnan* hates my guts for talking about his land deals."

The loss of farmland is only the latest of many waves of change that must eventually

▼ **Akha woman
of Mae Poen**

lead to the complete breakdown of the village.

Akoh has lived in *Baan* Mae Poen since it was an isolated, jungle settlement more then 30 years ago. He finds it painful to watch the crumbling of his village and his cherished traditions.

"Before, we never had problems of rice shortages. We never had to buy food, because there was lots of it in the forest. Things have changed so much since the forests went."

The hilltribe villagers resent being blamed for the denuded mountains.

"We hill people cleared the forest only for farming. We never felled trees to sell as the lowlanders who came up here did," says Atoloh. "If anything, they should be equally to blame."

Hunger is now a part of their life. A reservoir has been built nearby, flooding part of their farmland. No compensation was paid, because the hilltribes are considered illegal residents of the country.

Government officials came to set up a temporary school and development centre in the village to make the hill people feel Thai. The school is now abandoned, so the children have to walk across the mountain to attend the nearest school there.

One result has been that the young Akhas no longer wear their traditional clothes. They speak Thai fluently and their dream is to live

"When I'm dead and gone, our traditions will be gone with me."

▼ Akha woman
of Mae Poen

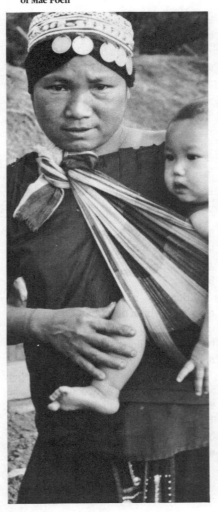

like the people they see on television.

Akoh, as village master of the animistic Akha ceremonies, watches all this with a frown.

"The young are no longer paying attention to their traditions. Half of us have already converted to Christianity. The rest might become Buddhists. The young look down on our ways.

"It saddens me to think that when I'm dead and gone, our traditions will be gone with me."

With the loss of the forest and the village's exotic culture, *Baan* Mae Poen no longer sees the tourist visitors who looked as if they had come from another world with their strange skins, hair colours and unintelligible speech.

Apart from the amusement of seeing such strange-looking people, Akoh says the villagers got nothing from tourism.

"They just came and went. Nothing in our life changed. All we could sell them was our old, traditional headgear. I can't show you what it's like, because there isn't any left now. These days, we cannot afford to make headgear with its silver coins for decoration. We have to use Thai baht coins instead."

As the village went into decline, the young Akha girls left, one by one, to work as prostitutes in the lowlands. They are considered exotic merchandise in the sex business.

The boys left to work in the city or on fishing trawlers.

"We want to have Thai nationality, but we just keep on waiting."

▼ **Children of**
Mae Poen

Guay, a middle-aged peasant, slowly edges into the conversation. In his hand is a picture of his son, who disappeared more than five years ago.

"Can you please find my son for me?" he pleads. "He was working on a trawler and then he disappeared. I'm afraid he has drowned."

Atoloh sighs with frustration. The young leader blames the mishaps that have befallen the young Akha people on the hill people's lack of legal citizenship.

"The authorities keep telling me they want us to be Thai, but their actions do not match their words. We want to have Thai nationality, but we just keep on waiting and waiting.

"Without the Thai ID card, we are trapped. We can't move around, except in constant fear of being arrested.

"Without that card, we can't get proper jobs. We can't get the same wages as the low-landers. The children cannot continue their studies after secondary school.

"The only job for the girls is prostitution and for the boys, dangerous, low-paid labouring, but when the family is hungry, you simply have no choice." Resentment is apparent in Atoloh's voice.

Ti, a young Akha man in a synthetic leather jacket, joins in.

"I want to have a good job. I want to have the same rights as others," he says. "I want to be able to complain to the authorities when we are bullied. All those things are impossible, because we don't have ID cards.

"We cannot leave home because of this. And things at home are so disheartening.

"Before, when there were girls in the village, we felt we had to be good and to work hard for the ones we loved.

"Now, the courting ground has long been haunted. Without the girls, we turn to opium for consolation. We need it to forget our worries.

"We are frustrated and bored. I see no hope left for us." ∎

Traditions resist change

◄ *Mae* Kamkai
Sitthiya

Time crawls at *Baan* Puang, a mist-shrouded village nestling in the hills of Lamphun province. But probably not for much longer.

"The giant spider's web has enfolded our village. So have the empty paths with no people on them, only worms," says *Mae* Kamkai Sitthiya, a middle-aged farmer talking about an old prophecy.

The cobweb, she explains, is the electricity cables that came to the village last year, bringing Bangkok and the modern world as close as the push of a button on a television set. The empty path is the road, recently laid to connect the village to the outside world. The worms are the curving tracks that cars leave behind on the path.

"The prophecy foretells a time when people have magic ears and eyes. And look what we have now - televisions and radios. Things are really coming true," she says in her melodious northern dialect which rings with conviction.

An ancient prophecy, omens of doom and eventual salvation by a new prophet are still taken seriously at *Baan* Puang, as are other northern traditions which are dying elsewhere in the region.

Hidden in the embrace of green mountains, *Baan* Puang with its traditional way of life still going strong gives a glimpse of what life in a self-contained, northern community used to be like before the modern cash economy entered it.

In the cool morning mist, *Baan* Puang is a picture of idyllic peace and serenity. The path leading to the village winds through golden ricefields. Dewdrops glitter on the blades of grass like diamonds. The only sound breaking the silence is the singing of a stream, its humming a constant reassurance of nature's abundance in the area.

"Most of us are lucky enough to grow sufficient rice to last the whole year," says village leader *Poh* Srimek Inmanee. "But our loyalty to the old ways has united us as well, and unity is important if we want to improve and protect our livelihood against outside forces."

Baan Puang's pulse is still very much governed by a belief in a hierarchy of spirits whose slightest change of mood can cause turbulence in one's body or family, in the community or in nature.

The biggest spirit in the vicinity is *Phii Hong*, whose residence has been built as big as a real house. It is surrounded by four*rai* of lush, green forest which, if it were not for fear of the spirit, axes would long since have felled.

At the entrance to the village, the home of *Phii Sua Baan*, the village spirit, stands regally on a mound beneath the shade of towering trees. One stops immediately to pay

of reciprocity be-
tween villagers must
be strictly observed
as well to ward off
unnecessary wrath.

"Traditions
keep us from going
astray. They hold us
together," says
farmer Srimek, pride
evident in his voice.

For example,
ao moe, the tradi-
tional practice of
taking turns working
in each other's
ricefields at planting

respect before entering his fiefdom of some
90 families. As one makes a *wai* towards his
miniature wooden house, one is unknow-
ingly taught the virtue of humility and respect
for time and place, without which social harmony cannot exist.

To restore harmony and keep the *Phii
Sua Baan, Phii Hong* and the *Phii Pu Ya*, the
ancestral spirits, happy takes more than intri-
cate ceremonies, although they are indispensable.

Quarrels among siblings and neighbours
are frowned upon, because they are believed
to make the spirits angry and liable to cause
illness or crop failure as punishment. The rule

and harvesting times, is still the norm in *Baan*
Puang, although it has been replaced by hired
wage labourers in other villages.

"The old way is good because our
ricefields are too small for us to hire labourers.
We simply cannot afford it," explains *Mae*
Kamkai. "People in Bangkok cannot depend
on one another, so they depend on money.
People in the countryside like us don't have
money. That's why we have to depend on one
another."

Kinship is the peasants' main social security system which has been kept intact by
the *Phii Pu Ya*, the ancestral spirit system
which divides *Baan* Puang into seven clans,

"People in the countryside don't have money, so we have to depend on one another."

▼ Puang villager
tending a kitchen
garden

taking matriarchal lineage.

"These ancestral spirits keep us together," says the matron Kamkai, whose home is used as the base of her clan's spirit house.

"All members of the clan, even if they live far apart from each other, are still considered relatives who have to help one another. Annual offerings to the clan's spirit also turn those who might otherwise have been strangers into family members," she says.

People in the same clan not only have a responsibility to help each other, but also the privilege of offering criticism which, from an "outsider", might cause anger and resentment.

Mae Kamkai also praises their spiritualism for helping protect women's dignity.

In courtship, it is considered *phid phii*, or upsetting the spirits, for a man to take advantage of a woman. If he does so, he is required to pay compensation or agree to marriage.

If a relationship becomes regular, the girl's parents may call on the boy's parents to determine their son's intentions. If the boy continues to see the girl, it means marriage. If he wavers, he must pay a large forfeit.

▼ **Puang villagers**

Even now, cautious tradition still demands that visitors of a different sex must stay in separate houses when they spend a night in the village, unless they are man and wife.

"Men and women too close together is like *krang klai fai, khai klai daed* - when varnish is left near a fire or sealing-wax in the sun, something is bound to happen. But our ancestors have designed a way to keep things in line," says the matron.

If the boy is from another village, it is tradition for the girl's family to visit his place to find out about his background.

"It doesn't matter if he's poor. All we're afraid of is that he might be one of the *phii pop* family," says *Mae* Kamkai, referring to village outcasts who are believed to be possessed by evil spirits.

"Luckily, there are few *phii pop* left. They can't stay in the villages, and I heard that most of them now stay in one place built by the Christian priests," she says with relief evident in her voice.

Adultery may infuriate the spirits, but *Mae* Kamkai has another explanation for the necessity of monogamy.

"How can poor people afford two wives? They can't even afford one," she chuckles. "Besides, wives have to work equally hard in the fields. Only the rich can fool around."

Aside from fear of the netherworld, the villagers' explanations of what has kept the village together for centuries attest to the fact that traditions, like inventions, are brought about by necessity.

"The dam across the river is the backbone of our village. We've got to unite and work together to keep it in good repair. Without the dam, we're finished," says *Poh* Srimek.

The River Li is the only source of water within a few kilometres of *Baan* Puang, but it lies much lower than the village. One cannot help being awed by the tenacity and inventiveness of those who first tamed the swift-running waters, so that they might be drawn up to the farmers' fields all year round.

The dam used to be made from thousands of timbers tied together. The villagers had to spend many months a year repairing and maintaining it.

"The dam often succumbed to the fierce currents. When that happened, it meant working day and night, cutting new timbers and transporting them with the help of elephants to the site. Men and women worked together, racing against time, because our livelihood of rice farming was at stake," recalls *Poh* Srimek.

The need to maintain the dam gave birth

▼ *Poh* **Gaew**
  Wongjand

to the villagers' own system of water management and leadership, based on democracy
and justice.

"Without the dam master, our village
would be in chaos," explains Srimek, looking
respectfully at the white-haired *Poh* Gaew
Wongjand, *Baan* Puang's dam master.

According to this system, each farmer
must put in time to repair the dam, the amount
of which is determined by the size of his
ricefields. The dam master, elected annually
by the villagers, is in charge of sharing out the

water fairly and supervising repair work.
Absenteeism or theft of water are punished,
with no exceptions.

"The dam master must be a man of
integrity and guts to keep the rules and trust of
the villagers," says Srimek, while the dam
master, a man of large build with a warm smile
and eyes that show his power, sits in respect-
ful silence.

As their forebears tamed the river's tor-
rents that have fed the village for generations,
so today's villagers must face the fiercer cur-

"We can't stop change. We just have to be careful not to let things happen too fast."

rents of modernity and progress.

Change, for better or for worse, is knocking at the village's door, bringing with it new problems that defy old solutions.

The wooden dam was replaced a few years ago with a cement one. The villagers felt that the old dam demanded more attention than they were able to give. They said they needed more time to work on their farms to meet more pressing needs for cash.

The cement dam, however, blocks the passage of silt, which accumulates in front of it, clogging up the irrigation reservoir. Fish and shrimps, which used to be abundant there, have disappeared.

The ties of traditional relationships have loosened as villagers spend less time together working on the dam.

With the excitement of city life dancing across their television screens every night, the repetitious rhythms of life in the countryside, which provided villagers with a sense of continuity and security, now begin to weigh heavily.

The temple is nearly empty. The only monk has automatically become abbot, even though he is only 23 years old.

"We can't stop change. We just have to be careful not to let things happen too fast," says Srimek.

But just that morning, the village had been hit by another wave in the flood of change.

A shock was felt throughout the village at the news that a young couple had been killed in a road accident, the first villagers to die in such a manner.

"We don't know what to do. It is so shocking. All we can do is to go to their families' houses to help out, as it is our tradition to do."

A village elder was sent to mediate between the parties involved in the accident. Word-of-mouth has it that the families have decided to let things pass.

Mae Kamkai sighs, nodding in agreement and understanding.

The driver of the car, a local policemen, is connected to one of the clans.

"We all know one another well in this small community. And we have to continue living together for a long time to come. No one wanted the accident to happen, including the driver. It's no use bearing grudges and sending him to prison. He's sorry for what happened, and the dead won't come back to life in any case."

The empty road with its worms has taken two lives. But just as *Mae* Kamkai finds hope in the coming of a new prophet, so she finds some consolation in this sad incident.

"At least they died together," the matron says earnestly. "That means that in their next life, they will be together once again." ∎

About the author

Sanitsuda Ekachai has been a reporter and feature writer with the *Bangkok Post,* Thailand's major English language daily newspaper, for seven years. She specialises in rural development, women's issues, Buddhism and the environment.

About the publisher

Thai Development Support Committee is a Thai non-governmental organisation (NGO). It was established in 1982 to coordinate and support the fledgling social development NGO movement in Thailand.

Its broad objective is to create awareness and understanding of the social development issues affecting communities in Thailand today such as farmers' debt, labour migration, landlessness, environmental degradation, deforestation, eviction of slum dwellers, prostitution and child labour. The aim of its work is to increase moral and financial support for NGOs working with the poorest and most disadvantaged people in the country who are affected by these issues.

It produces a quarterly publication in English, *Thai Development Newsletter,* and other media to cover these and other issues from an NGO perspective.

Thai Development Support Committee worked with Sanitsuda Ekachai to produce the articles in *Behind the Smile: Voices of Thailand.*

For more information about NGO and development activities in Thailand, contact:
Thai Development Support Committee
530 Soi St Louis 3
South Sathorn Road
Yannawa
Bangkok 10120
THAILAND